D1596227

# ALIVE

To Gwen:

Enjoy finding and
staying ALIVE!
Much love ♡
Ken

# KARIN LEHMANN

# ALIVE

A Practical Guide
to Get Out of Your Head
and into Your Heart

AUTHOR'S NOTE: Throughout this book I have drawn on examples from the clients in my programs and workshops. However, to protect their privacy and ensure confidentiality, I have changed their names, descriptions, and other identifying characteristics. I am profoundly grateful for their trust in me.

Printed in the United States of America
Cover design by Uta Culemann-Ritke

ISBN-13: 978-0692287941
ISBN-10: 0692287949

*This book is dedicated to my parents. Their unwavering belief instilled in me the courage to follow my inner voice and explore life with passion and confidence.*

# Contents

# INTRODUCTION

*Have the courage to follow your heart and intuition. They somehow already know what you truly want to become. Everything else is secondary.*

—**Steve Jobs,** *Stanford commencement address*

## My Beginnings

It was a beautiful spring day in 1988 and I was 27 years old. I lived in a small village of fewer than 300 souls in the Black Forest area of Germany with my husband and our two small children. There were no stores, no school or post office, not even a single restaurant or bar. It was a quaint place surrounded by hills and pine trees with cows grazing in lush pastures. Most of my days were spent taking care of my kids, baking, cooking, and gardening while my husband worked for a local carpenter.

On that afternoon, I was strolling along the hillside pushing a baby carriage with my three-month-old daughter. My two-year-old son was skipping ahead and singing. I looked over the beautiful mountains and all of a sudden, something became exceedingly clear to me: this was not where I belonged. This was not the life I was born to live.

Standing there, I could feel a deep loneliness in my bones and a longing in my heart. I realized that while I loved my kids and husband, something profound was missing from my life. What was I doing here? I love people: being around them, observing them, talking to them, and discovering their stories. I love to be social and here I was, in this remote little village, completely removed from the rest of the world.

It was this small incident that marked the beginning of a journey that would take me to the center of who I am. At the time, I noticed only that a part of my soul was lying dormant—that something was missing. It was the first step of my search for completeness.

## Your Journey

Is it possible that you are at a similar place in your own life, with feelings and yearnings for something that you know is missing? Maybe you are wondering whether you are on track. Are you following your legend or are you way off your path? Is this as good as it gets, or is there still an adventure out there? Should you take the leap of faith and leave a mediocre job to find your true calling? Will you ever meet your soulmate and start a family?

Maybe you are tired of the role you have been playing in life: the good girl, the rebel, or perhaps the wallflower. Maybe you wish to break out of the mold—go wild, explore, break the rules, and be bold. Maybe you are happy with your life but you desire to reach even further, deeper, and tap into every aspect of your being.

Twenty-six years after that defining afternoon stroll in the Black Forest, I am here to tell you that you have to begin your quest. If you are persistently wondering yes or no, stay or go, high or low, then I say that you need to stop second-guessing yourself and start your journey.

It took me almost ten years to build up the courage to follow my dream and to find my true calling. My marriage had to fall apart, I had to move around the globe, and I lost all my money, before I was finally ready to listen to my heart. And while my journey has been an extraordinary adventure, it was at times painful, lonely, scary, and utterly unsettling.

It doesn't need to be this hard for you. Using the path outlined in this book, you can avoid most of the mistakes I made and start your own journey on the right foot—without missing out on all the exciting experiences along the way. If you have the courage to go for it wholeheartedly, it is going to be a wild trip—much better than any blockbuster movie or record-breaking TV show could ever be—because it is your life. What could be more thrilling than that?

# The Purpose of This Book

Understanding and looking deep into one's soul is a skill we are all born with, but few of us ever learn to develop it. Showing you how to understand yourself better and decipher your life's meaning is the purpose of this book.

Why is it so hard for most people to design and live a satisfying existence? Why do we feel so obligated to fit into a system that conflicts with our true nature, doing what others expect of us instead of following our heart's desire? Why is the path hidden from us, and why do we have such a difficult time finding our true calling?

The answers to these questions are surprisingly simple, yet few people have been able to find them. The importance of knowing your purpose and the joy that comes from living your passion has been addressed in countless articles, books, seminars, and discussions; so far, almost no one has been able to offer true and tested solutions.

*In this book, I give you the map, the step-by-step outline, to help you get to the core of who you are.*

You have special gifts. You have talents with which only you were born. The tools and exercises provided in this book will help you to accurately realize and use them. You will understand your motivations and map your way to a happier and brighter future—a future that is in tune with who you are and who you want to be.

Once you begin your journey, you will encounter many enlightening surprises. You will discover that your path has been outlined for you all along, hidden in plain sight, and that all you have to do is follow the signs. You will learn that by paying attention to your inner voice, you can access levels of joy and satisfaction that few people ever experience. And you will come to understand how truly magnificent and unabashedly happy you naturally are; to live in the realm of magic all you have to do is breathe, relax, and let go.

To get there, you have to put in the work. You have to embrace new tools and unlearn the patterns and unproductive habits that have gotten you where you are now. Unfortunately, there isn't a red or blue pill to get you faster results. You won't just make the changes by reading this book, either. You have to learn and practice and then, learn and practice again. And just as with any other new skill, it takes time to master it.

Is the journey worth it? You bet. If you want to live your dream and inspire people with your passion, I recommend you start right away. Here are some of the perks you will experience along the way:

- You become happier and more relaxed; you experience ease and calmness. This is your natural state.

- You stop searching and start attracting to your life the things you want. You experience synchronicity and flow.

- You become more confident and are able to take more risks. Women often tell me that they are risk averse—using your brilliance gives you the courage to take bigger steps.

- You become more beautiful and magnetic. You start to look and feel younger and more attractive.

- And finally, knowing what you love to do, you will be able to build a lucrative business, attract the right career and create a lifestyle based on your passion. This connects you with a community of like-minded people and brings you the happiness for which you have been searching.

It is surprising and at times shocking to grasp your own greatness. And then again, it's the most natural thing in the world. By the time you finish this book, you will understand yourself and others in a whole new way—for you will have discovered the secrets, which most people don't know, about finding and living your destiny.

# How to Use This Book

This book is for you. I have poured everything I know about personal transformation into it: tools, exercises, stories, examples, role-plays, and questionnaires.

Make this book your best friend, your own personal advisor, to whom you turn in times of change. Step by step, I will walk you through the process of self-discovery, just as if you were sitting across from me in a personal consultation.

In **Chapter 1,** I let you in on the three secrets that prevent most people from actualizing their true potential. You will understand why it has been so difficult for you to put a finger on your own gifts and passions. You will discover how you got off track and realize what has been holding you back. Until now.

In **Chapter 3,** you go on a treasure hunt to find your unique gifts and passions. You explore and rediscover the ingredients for your happiness and satisfaction. You are introduced to my cellular transformation tools and learn to accurately read your identity blueprint. Exercises and role-plays will help you along the way.

In **Chapter 7**, you create an action plan to actualize your dream. Knowing your gifts and passions is the first step—applying yourself and living your adventure is the ultimate goal.

**The stories** provide you with examples of other people's journeys. Discovering how others dealt with situations similar to yours helps you to understand and accept what's going on in your own life.

**The exercises** help you explore. You acquire new tools and life skills—and understand what's unique and special about you.

**The tools** are transformational and can be applied to all areas of your life: parenting, relationships, business, family, and positively affect how you communicate and interact with others.

**The role-plays** require the help of a friend or partner.

**The mantras** help you to integrate and digest the information presented. Use them as a guide.

**Recommendation:** Take your time and enjoy the process. This is your life and it does not need to be rushed. If you can stay curious throughout, applying what is true for you and discarding what is not, you will get the most out of this book.

**Warning!** You see the best results when you apply the tools and work on yourself until it becomes second nature. Endurance and patience are an integral part of this process. Unfortunately, I have seen people give up too early, sometimes just a few steps before arriving at their destination.

So, hang in there and let the journey begin.

---

### Learning Defined

True learning happens when we get involved and explore. For some this means to read and digest information by pondering, reflecting, and talking about it. Others learn best by engaging in diverse exercises, questionnaires, role-plays, and intakes. If you learn easiest by listening to the material, I will be offering an audio version of the book.

---

# YOU WERE BORN WITH A GIFT

*The best way to make your dreams come true
is to wake up.*

—**Paul Valéry**, French poet

What is a gift? Is it something you learn? Is it what you are good at? Is it your passion? And, most important, how do you find it?

In my early thirties, these questions started to haunt me. I had ignored the little voice that told me something was missing. I had tried to live my life as well as I knew how to by being a good mom to my kids and a devoted wife to my husband. At this point, however, things started to fall apart. I had turned 33 and my marriage was crumbling.

I realized that I was about to become a single mom with two small kids to take care of and that I had no idea what I was good at or what I wanted to do with my life. I was completely in the dark about my talents and I was really scared.

Due to fortunate circumstances—or a higher intervention—I met someone during that time who became my coach and mentor. He showed me that I had a special gift of listening to people, which allowed me to perceive their dreams and desires.

This came as a total shock to me. I didn't think I was good with people; I was actually rather shy. My mentor encouraged me to polish and deepen my gift, which I did. As a result, I began to look deep into people's souls and their core essence.

I learned to see more. I became able to see how people weren't their true selves and how by creating fake characters or putting on a show, they tried to hide their insecurities. I was able to see the bigger picture: who they were and, more important, who they wanted to be.

As I started to work with people, my life expanded. I was able to do what I had always wanted to do, but didn't think was possible. I moved to the United States with my two little kids. I built my consulting firm, sharing my expertise with men and women in the United States, Europe, and South America. I found my dream partner and now live in southern California, a place where I feel at home.

Maybe you already know your unique talents and use them every day. If so, you are lucky. It is a blessing to know exactly what you were born to do. For you, this book can provide a valuable tool to dig even deeper and to understand yourself and others on the most intimate soul level.

If you don't have a clue about your gifts, don't worry. Every single person has a special purpose. And just as your fingerprints are completely unique among the 7.16 billion people on this planet, so are your personal traits. There is not one person like you, with the same specific abilities and talents.

You might ask yourself, "If we are all so unique, why is it so difficult for most people to find their special qualities? Why don't we all just tap into our passion and apply ourselves to the things we love?" You are about to find out why.

---

### Your Passions and Gifts Defined

Passions and gifts are two terms I use in this book a lot, so I want make a few distinctions:

Your passions are the activities you engage in when you forget yourself. For example, when you sit down with a good book that completely captivates you. You forget the world around you while you are reading.

Your gifts are the natural talents with which you are born. They are your ability to see beauty in the most uncommon places, to concoct sublime pastries, or to cut someone's hair with that special flair. For you, it is not a big deal, yet nobody else does it quite like you do.

When you combine your passions with your gifts, your true essence, the artist and creator in you, comes to light and your life starts to flow with magic and ease.

**Important:** Engaging in your gifts is not hard, but this does not mean that polishing them is not hard work.

Masters in their fields, such as author Stephen King or basketball legend Michael Jordan, say the same thing about using their crafts: it requires relentless practice. Stephen King writes a minimum of ten pages every day, Sundays and holidays included. Michael Jordan threw hoop after hoop until he could do it with his eyes closed. You have to be passionate about what you do to keep up with such a rigorous practice.

# CHAPTER 1
# The Three Secrets
# No One Ever Told You

*All of the drama humans suffer is the result of believing in lies, mainly about ourselves. The first lie we believe in is I am not: I am not the way I should be, I am not perfect. The truth is that every human is born perfect because only perfection exists.*

—**Don Miguel Ruiz**, *The Voice of Knowledge*

The first step in living a significant life is to understand what truly makes you tick. And that's where most people get stuck.

In this chapter, I am letting you in on three little secrets that prevent most people from understanding who they are. You might think this must be a life-shaking revelation, but in reality, it's quite simple.

# Secret One:
# You Can't See Your Own Brilliance

Lisa came to me because she couldn't figure out what she wanted to do with her life. "So many things excite me," she told me. "One day I want to start a bed and breakfast and the next day I want to open a pet business. My problem is that I can't make up my mind. Maybe I have attention deficit disorder?" After talking for a little while, it became clear that Lisa was good at many things that weren't her passions. It was easy for her to organize an event or plan a trip for friends, but neither one inspired her.

I noticed that Lisa was dressed in a beautiful and creative way and that it was fun to look at her. "Do you like clothes?" I asked her. She perked up immediately. "It's actually one of my secret addictions," she responded smiling. "I love shopping and have to stop myself from not going overboard." She went on to tell me that she could spend hours looking through fashion magazines and browse local boutiques without getting tired.

Lisa has a knack for making the world around her beautiful, yet she thought it was something everyone did. She had even convinced herself that if she wasn't careful she'd turn into a shopaholic. "Doesn't every woman love shopping and dressing up?" she asked. I told her no, that many women had a hard time knowing what looked good on them. "Seriously?" she asked, with an incredulous look on her face.

**Here is the deal:** The reason you don't tap into your passion and apply your gifts is that you simply don't recognize them. You can't see your own brilliance and you don't understand how unique you are. Because your talents are innate and you use them every single day, to you, your greatness is completely normal.

Maybe you see wonderful colors and beauty when you are in nature and you love to write about it. Or, maybe you like to cook, and for you every trip to the grocery store is an exciting opportunity to dream up new recipes.

To you, this doesn't seem extraordinary. You actually believe that other people are just like you. That they too enjoy exploring nature or cooking nice meals; that they want to become famous musicians or celebrated writers. Not everyone, however, has the same gifts and desires you do. Believing otherwise is the single reason so many talents are squandered and dreams buried. Most of us are convinced that our talents are not as good as those of others and that we don't have what it takes to stand out.

**Here is the dilemma:** It is as if you are stuck *inside* a box and the instructions on how to get out are written on the *outside* of the box. You can't see your own brilliance. Only other people can see you for who you are.

Unfortunately, they rarely point your brilliance out to you.

## Secret Two: You Have All the Answers

Let me guess, growing up, you didn't learn how to trust your talents. Your teachers didn't encourage you to follow your curiosity and you never found out how to understand and read your own incomparable intelligence. On the contrary, early on you figured out that too much joy for life was getting you into trouble and that following reason, instead of passion, was safer when making decisions.

What you didn't notice was that every time you refused to follow your innate curiosity, you lost some of your spark. Every time you did not listen to your heart, your inner glow diminished. By following everyone else's advice, you disconnected from your soul.

*Over time, you stopped trusting your inspiration and forgot that the answers to your happiness lie within you.* You learned to fit in and the more you fit in, the more you got stuck and the less exciting life became.

A few years ago, Ben came to see me. He had a solid career, was happily married, and had two wonderful kids. It looked like he had it all together. After talking to him for a little while, I asked him how I could help. He hesitated and then burst out, "It looks like I have everything I could have ever wished for. I love my wife and kids, and I have a great job. For some reason, though, I am not as happy as you might suspect."

In all the years I had worked with people, I had learned not to suspect anything, but I didn't tell him this. "It's as if something is missing," he went on. "And the older I get, the more it feels as if I am on the wrong track."

We talked about his hidden dreams and desires and came up with a few things he always wanted to do, but hadn't. For some reason, nothing really hit home. "Do you like music?" I asked him. He looked at me surprised. "Why would you ask that?" He sounded a bit guarded. "Well, you remind me of Elton John," I told him.

I look for patterns of resonance and the spark in someone's eyes when working with people. And sometimes I just follow a hunch. Looking at Ben, I had been thinking of Elton John, so I threw it out there to see where it landed.

Ben looked baffled and started to tear up. After a moment of silence he said, "I don't know how you came up with this, but Elton John is one of my favorite musicians. I always wanted to be like him." "Do you play music?" I asked him. "No," he said. "I never thought I would be good enough." Just like that, he had shut down a dream; he had stopped trusting that he had all the answers to find his happiness.

Don't think this is an exception. Most people stop following their inner voice and never actualize their true potential. Not everyone, however, is as stuck as Ben was. He had no clue that music was part of his passion and because he was not nurturing it, he felt incomplete.

Losing touch with your innate talents happens gradually. As a kid, you are open and your curiosity leads the way to your gifts. Yet, growing up, you learn to shut down and your inner fire dwindles. In the process, you forget who you are and you stop trusting your own instincts.

# Secret Three:
# Logic Doesn't Lead to Happiness

Because you don't trust your inner voice and are stuck in the proverbial box for making important life decisions, you end up following the wrong clues when it comes to finding your purpose. Instead of listening to your heart, you follow logic and rational thought to find your personal path.

The challenge is to realize and accept how amazing you are. You have no idea what you add to the world. You have been misled from a young age and never learned to understand your brilliance.

What you did learn is how to be smart. You know how to find the answers to the most complicated questions, come up with expert solutions, and approach life from a practical point of view. You learned to be efficient at solving problems, and are now trying to figure out who you are by using your brain.

The tricky part is that you can't find your life's meaning by thinking about it. You can't find what you love with a questionnaire or test.

But isn't that what you have been doing? Have you not learned that you can resolve anything by thinking really hard about it? Unfortunately, in this case that strategy won't work. Your essence isn't a problem you can figure out in your head. You have to go deeper than that. You have to look into your heart and listen for your innermost desires to find your life's meaning.

And that is exactly what you never learned to do.

How do you follow your heart? How do you find your own unique path, the reason you were born and the purpose you are here to fulfill?

If you are longing to find the answers to those essential questions, skip ahead to Chapter 3, "Read Your Identity Blueprint."

Otherwise, find out in more detail how you get pulled off your path and gradually disengage from your inner truth in the following chapter. Because this can get a bit serious at times, I caution you to keep your sense of humor. There is nothing wrong with being stuck and losing sight of your brilliance. On the contrary, understanding life's polarities helps you to be a more compassionate and complete person. You know that with light, there is darkness; and without sadness, there is no happiness.

*Mantra*—Breathe, relax, and let go. You have a purpose, a unique calling. In this book, you will find out exactly what that is. For now, just enjoy the ride and trust that the answers will be revealed when you are ready.

# CHAPTER 2
## How You Got
## Where You Are Now

*About the process of growing up…*

*What follows is tragic. We stop risking for fear of making mistakes, fear of not fitting in, fear of being embarrassed or humiliated by saying the "wrong" thing. Our instinctive joy and boundless enthusiasm are replaced by playing it safe and looking good. Our spontaneity deserts us, and with it much of our natural creativity. Predictability replaces passion. We learn to reveal very little of who we really are and what we really feel. We sell the richness of our passionate birthright for the security of this burdensome thing called our "image." It weighs us down like a suit of medieval armor, restricting our every move, sapping our vitality and aliveness. We wander through life on automatic pilot, controlled by the need to live up to the false image that we invented.*

—Robert White, *Living an Extraordinary Life*

# How You Learned to Shut Down

You are born happy. As a baby, you know no boundaries. You are bursting with energy and ready to explore the world around you at full force. You play, you follow your curiosity, and you live in a state of constant wonder.

Between the age of one and two, the word you hear most often is "no." No, you can't have this. No, you can't do that. Don't climb up there. Don't open the door. Don't put that in your mouth. Don't make a mess with your food.

Rules are important; don't get me wrong. The tricky part is to use them without losing your curiosity at the same time.

You learn to fit in, you learn to behave. Soon you find out that loving everybody unconditionally can hurt when people don't love you back. So you close off your heart just a little bit and love becomes conditional.

Going to school is a whole different experience. All of a sudden, you have to sit still all day and find answers to problems. You would much rather run around and experience the world with your senses, but instead you get conditioned to experience it through your mind. You learn quickly. Knowing the right answer gets rewards, so you get really good at finding out what the teacher wants you to know.

You learn how to compete. Who has the better grades? Who is the strongest, fastest, or prettiest? Instead of playing together, we start playing against one another.

During puberty, you don't ask the questions you really want to ask, for people tend to act strange when you do. So you shut down your natural curiosity some more.

Finally, around the time you leave school, life flips upside down and you enter the world of worry, fear, and scarcity. You find out that the things don't run the way you were told they do. Your strong trust that everything will turn out the way it's supposed to and that life is meant to be an exciting adventure starts to vanish.

From that moment on, you make decisions based on fear and life becomes a struggle. You compromise; you enter a career that doesn't completely fulfill you; you get used to a life that lacks passion, and slowly you forget whom you really are. You tell yourself you are doing well and you enjoy the stability and safety that your life provides—but somewhere deep down you are waiting for something to change. You secretly know that life isn't what you thought it would be and you start asking yourself "Is that all there is?"

For many this is a turning point. It is the moment when you ask yourself what your mission is in life and how to fulfill it. Experiencing the darker side of life has helped you to grow deep roots. Now it is time to find your light and purpose.

ACTION STEP

Take some of your baby pictures and compare them to pictures of yourself today. How are they different? Apart from being older, how has your face changed? What emotions do you see in your baby pictures and what emotions do you see to today?

# You Are Not Who You Think You Are

Not only do we learn how to shut down while growing up, we also figure out that who we are is not enough. One of our deepest desires is to be accepted and loved for whom we are, so we start to make adjustments to our personalities in an effort to become the persons that others will accept.

Unless you are brought up in an environment that allows you to explore and follow your natural curiosity, you learn to bend your character a little as you get older, trying to win the approval of your friends and family. You start to withhold your passion, tell others what they want to hear, and, in general, lose sight of who you are and what your unique purpose in life really is. You play it safe.

What you might not realize is that gradually you create a personality that's not you. And you build your whole life around it.

When I was a kid, I decided that because I was not adorable (clearly, my little sister owned that attribute), I would be reliable, trustworthy, and dependable. It was an act. I had made up my mind that since I couldn't be charming and playful, I would impress people by being a responsible know-it-all. I got positive feedback which did not make me happy because my act did not fit my essence.

"Karin is so responsible and mature for her age, you can always rely on her to get things done." I hated it. I did not want to be mature and reliable. I wanted to be cute and adorable. Yet, I kept up appearances because it got me praise and attention. Over time, I started to believe in my fake personality and accepted my act. I thought of myself as reliable, yet boring, responsible, and serious.

This pretty much sums up what happens to most of us. We turn into someone we are not. And because our fake persona doesn't fit our true character, we don't get much praise, appreciation, or acknowledgment. The feedback we do get annoys us, rather than inspires and uplifts us.

The good news is that the world of joy and magic you experienced as a kid is still there, all around you.

You just lost touch with it by focusing too much on your problems or playing a role that isn't who you really are. On rare occasions, when you forget yourself and get lost in something you enjoy, you get glimpses of how life could be.

How do you access that world of ease and wonder? How do you leave the reality of fear and worry behind? That's what we explore in the remaining chapters of this book.

## ACTION STEP

Think back and recall instances in your life when you made up your mind to put on an act that wasn't you. Maybe you got attention for being a troublemaker or for always being proper. Maybe you were punished for something you didn't do and adopted an attitude of defiance. One of my clients told me that his mom always pointed out how well behaved he was, and because he did not want to upset her he kept up the good boy act, when all he really wanted was to be bold and daring.

Once you understand the instances that shaped who you are today, think about a role you'd rather play. How do you want to be perceived? What character inspires you? If you could be anybody, who would you like to be?

# Life Questionnaire

Take a few moments to answer the following Life Questionnaire. It will help you to gain clarity about your life at this point in time. Be spontaneous with your answers and have fun with the process.

1. **Throughout your day, when do you experience the most joy?**

    Circle one or more of the following answers:

    o   At work: I love what I do, and when I am focused, I feel exhilarated and excited!

    o   When I am creative: That's when I forget everything around me and time flies.

    o   Exercising or spending time in nature.

    o   When I am with my partner, kids, family, and friends.

    o   Being quiet, relaxing, doing nothing, daydreaming, or meditating.

    o   Other: _____

2. **Briefly, describe your most important qualities.** These can be positive or negative. Your weaknesses can also be your biggest strengths.

For example: Being critical. When applied toward people, this can be a weakness. When used to improve systems and structures, however, it becomes an asset.

_____

_____

_____

_____

_____

_____

3. **What area of your life causes you the most pain right now?**

   Circle one or more of the following answers.

   o   Work / career / business
   o   Intimate relationships (or lack thereof)
   o   Inability to stay on track with my goals
   o   Overall stress
   o   Money issues
   o   Not enough time for the fun things in life
   o   Other: _____

4.  **What are the activities that make you forget everything around you?**

    For example: Can you dance for hours without noticing how time passes? Or, do you like reading, taking pictures, cooking, shopping, visiting friends, etc.?

    _____

    _____

    _____

    _____

    _____

    _____

5.  **If you had more time (to do anything), how would you spend it?**
    Circle one or more of the following answers:

    o   I'd love to travel more and explore other cultures.
    o   Being creative: writing, photography, painting, gardening, or just dreaming things up.
    o   I'd like to party more and meet new people.
    o   I would love to spend more time with my family.
    o   My health: If I had more time, I would eat better and exercise more.

    o   Other: _____

6. **What time in your life has been the happiest? What were you doing?**

_____

_____

_____

_____

_____

_____

7. **How do you respond when faced with major life challenges?**

Circle one or more of the following answers:
- I don't experience life challenges.
- I hide under the covers until the worst is over.
- Challenges stimulate me, the bigger, the better.
- By screaming and throwing a fit.
- When the going gets tough, the great ones party.
- I get tired or depressed.
- Other: _____

8. Imagine living your life without limitations—you can have anything you want and live the lifestyle that makes you happiest—what would you do?

Go for it, dream BIG!

_____

_____

_____

_____

_____

_____

9. Do you have a clear vision for your life and future?

Circle one or more of the following answers:

○ Right now I am exploring my options in life and don't have a clear vision.

○ I feel really stuck and don't have a vision for my life. I would like some clarity and focus.

○ I am clear about my dream life but don't know how to put it into action.

○ Yes, I have a clear plan and vision for my future.

○ Other: _____

*Mantra*—Before you move on, take a minute to accept who you are now and the life you have created for yourself. Everything is perfect the way it is. From there, you can work on making it better.

This is a good time to celebrate what you already have. Celebrate your courage to invite change. Celebrate your wins and your losses. Celebrate your dreams and your desires. And, most important, celebrate being you.

# REVEAL YOUR TRUE CALLING

*To find yourself, you have to lose yourself in something you love.*

—**Martin Sage**, business coach and author

Some people find their life's purpose by stumbling on it; others awaken to it through tragedy; some experience an epiphany or receive a distinct message from a higher source. Most people, however, wander around in the dark without a clear path to follow.

In this part of the book, I provide you with clearly defined, practical steps that will help you reveal your identity blueprint, your true personal calling. These steps are tried and proven and when combined will allow you to see your life in a new light. You will expand your awareness, see reality with more accuracy, and understand the reason you are here.

*These steps are the vehicle to your transformation.*

While the approach is simple, it will require adjustments to the way you perceive yourself and your role in life. To truly integrate the steps and transformation tools provided, you have to put in the time and discipline to learn, practice, and polish them.

# CHAPTER 3
# Read Your Identity Blueprint

Remember the three secrets I shared with you in Chapter 1 and the reason most people have such a hard time understanding their own brilliance?

This chapter provides a step-by-step approach, a road map to your life's purpose that up until now nobody has outlined for you. By following it, you are able to read your personal essence, unveil the secrets to your brilliance, and deeply connect with your soul. You will have your identity blueprint.

*I urge you to pay close attention, because this is where many self-help books and seminars fall short about this topic.*

While most people agree that finding your passion and knowing your true calling are essential for living a meaningful life, few provide practical tools of self-discovery.

# Follow the Fire Within

*For the past 33 years, I have looked in the mirror every morning and asked myself: "If today were the last day of my life, would I want to do what I am about to do today?" And whenever the answer has been "No" for too many days in a row, I know I need to change something.*

—**Steve Jobs,** *Stanford commencement address*

To find your gifts, to truly recognize your own brilliance, and to grasp the greatness with which you are born, you have to get out of your head.

You must sidestep your rational thought. Forget the ideas, the concepts, the opinions, and the arguments you have learned throughout your life. Dare to go deeper. Instead of listening to the voice of reason, learn to pay attention to the subtle clues of your heart; listen to your body and soul for the clues to your passion. To change the perception you have of yourself, you have to get in touch with the fire you are holding within, the spark that ignites you, which at this time might be burning low.

And that's exactly where things get tricky. How do you know when your heart is speaking and not your brain? How do you listen to the music of your soul? How can you be sure that the yearning to make delicate jewelry or to write a children's book is your passion speaking and not your mind playing tricks on you?

What clues and signs do you follow on your path to self-discovery? How can you distinguish between the voice in your head and the voice of your heart? Those and other essential questions are addressed and answered in this chapter, so you can decipher the signs that lead to your passion and gain confidence in following your heart.

Essentially, reading your identity blueprint consists of three steps:

1. *Listen to Aliveness*

2. *Gain Clarity*

3. *Make Adjustments*

Each step comes with a set of transformation tools that will make the process clear and easy to follow. By using the tools and following the steps, you are able to build a solid foundation from which to make your life's essential decisions. Using the steps as a guideline, the path in front of you becomes clear, and you can stop the guessing game of whether or not you are on the right track.

# Step One: Listen to Aliveness

## Transformation Tools

- Observation

- Curiosity

Finding out what sparks your inner fire and brings you alive is the first and fundamental step in reading your identity blueprint. Following your passion will help you recognize your brilliance and reveal what it is you long for in the depth of your being.

While this principle is simple—you are bursting with vitality or you are not—it can be hard to grasp. We are accustomed to follow logic rather than sparks of energy and vibrant connections when looking for answers to our life's path.

To find your unique qualities, you have to distinguish the activities that set your heart on fire. The ones that make your palms sweat, that create a sense of nervous excitement at the base of your spine and that light you up from head to toe.

*The first step on your path is to get out of your head and into your body.*

That is easier said than done. Most of us are efficient at living in our rational mind. We are stuck recycling old ideas, worrying about our future, and obsessing about the past. Seldom do we spend time in the here and now, attuned to what is going on within us and around us. The same is true when we talk to people. We share rehashed ideas and outdated concepts; we convey our opinions and judgments and are unaware of the fact that our conversations lack enthusiasm and inspiration.

Every once in a while someone touches us in a way that deeply resonates and leaves us energized and excited. In those rare instances, we wonder, *What's possible? Could life be like that?* A glimpse of truth and essence pierces through the bubble of fear and insecurity with which we have surrounded ourselves and reaches into our heart. In those moments, we get a sense of a different kind of reality, one that's vibrant, inspiring, and utterly alive.

That is the reality you will learn about in this chapter. For now, whenever you encounter one of those special moments of someone deeply touching you, stop talking and pay attention. Someone's heart is speaking to you! And if you want to get infected with its enthusiasm, listen and stop putting out the fire.

Listening to aliveness, first in other people and then in yourself, will allow you to look past outside appearances, social façades, and carefully constructed roles that you have put together to protect yourself from being hurt. These fake acts keep you at a distance from others—and ultimately from yourself.

If you learn to accurately read and respond to your heart's desires, you can carefully peel away layers and layers of pressure, angst, false self-perception, worry, disbelief, and low self-esteem that you learned and accepted as your identity.

Your brilliance communicates with you through aliveness. Whenever your heart speaks, you feel it in your body; when your soul stirs, it touches you at the core of your being.

## HOW IT WORKS

When your natural wisdom speaks through your body, your level of aliveness increases; you smile, your eyes sparkle, and you feel a surge of energy; *you light up*.

*Observation* and *curiosity* are the transformation tools that will help you with this step. By observing yourself and others, you become aware of subtle shifts in energy, moments that increase or decrease your aliveness; instances that inspire you or turn you off; thoughts that make you tense or relaxed.

At first, it is easier to watch these differences in others. When is someone getting more excited? What topics stir a person's desires? Which ones turn them off?

To do this, you have to shift your attention away from the voice in your mind and pay attention to the sensations in your body. Observe how your senses respond to your environment, to people, and to situations. Notice when your body feels alive and vibrant versus becoming tired, sluggish, and slow. Realize how certain situations cause you stress, while others put you at ease.

**Let's do a little demonstration:** Take a moment, sit back in your chair, and imagine running a hot bath after a long day, lighting some candles and putting on your favorite music. Got it? Now pay attention to what happens to your body when you think about it. What sensations do you feel? Are you getting more relaxed or tenser? Are you breathing deeper or shallower? Are you experiencing joy or aggravation?

Now, imagine doing your taxes this weekend. Again, pay attention to what happens to you. How are the sensations in your body changing? Do you feel the same as before or different? If there is a difference, how does it feel? Is it putting you at ease or is it making you tenser?

What seems like a random response is actually your body showing you your inner vision. When you start paying attention to the moments that empower you and make you happy, they will lead you to the secrets of your heart and your identity blueprint. Combined, the pieces will add up to a puzzle containing the secrets to your special gifts, the things you are uniquely put on this Earth to do. It all starts with you paying attention to your energetic response mechanism, the stuff that lights your fire.

### Your Identity Blueprint Defined

Everything about you—the way you talk, the way you walk, the shape of your body, the style of your thinking, and the desire in your heart—all adds up to a set of unique qualities and gifts: Your identity blueprint. In unison with your mission and personal vision, they form the master plan for your life.

Let's add the second transformation tool to the process, curiosity, which to me is the magic ingredient. It keeps your observations fresh. Curiosity is the ability to look at the world through a lens of imagination, wonder, and delightful amazement. Without curiosity, you form opinions and come to conclusions. You lose your natural appreciation of the little mysteries of everyday life and take things for granted.

By adding curiosity to the process of reading aliveness, you avoid labeling what you are observing. With curiosity, you simply don't know, you have no answers, which is a blessing because it keeps you looking for more.

Physicist Albert Einstein once said, "Most people stop looking when they find the proverbial needle in the haystack. I would continue looking to see if there were other needles."

Curiosity is at the core of true learning. Little kids are immensely curious. They haven't yet learned how the world works and so they keep exploring at full force—without expecting a certain outcome.

*With curiosity, everything is possible.*

Let's see how curiosity contributes to the observation process. By paying attention to your environment, you notice that every time your boss leaves the office your aliveness increases and you relax. That's your observation. You are more relaxed without your boss being present at the office. Without curiosity, you might come up with the conclusion that you don't like your boss. Period; case closed; you have an answer.

Now, add curiosity to the mix. What else do you notice? Does your energy always shift with your boss coming to or leaving the office? How does your environment change with your boss in it? How does his presence affect your coworkers? How energized is your boss when he comes to work? Is he delighted with his job?

By adding curiosity to your observations, you expand them. In this scenario, many influences can cause a shift in your aliveness: maybe your boss doesn't like his job. Maybe your colleague is afraid of your boss. Maybe you have an issue with authority figures. Or, maybe it is none of the above and you have to keep observing.

With curiosity, you are open to any way your life wants to flow. Without it, you will keep getting stuck with answers, labels, and interpretations that might—or might not— be true.

Do you get a sense of how this works? If not, don't worry, we will keep practicing and reinforcing these tools throughout the book. There is an awareness exercise at the end of this chapter that will help you to practice using observation and curiosity to read people. In addition, you have an opportunity to review the art of reading aliveness in Chapter 4.

At this level of understanding your inner identity, three things will get in your way and hinder your progress: the voice of your rational mind, coming to conclusions, and making interpretations. I outline them under "Obstacles on Your Way" in the next chapter so you can avoid falling into their traps.

ACTION STEP
Before we move on to Step Two, let's practice what we have covered so far. The best way to do this is to go out

and observe people to find out what brings someone alive. You can do this in person, at a coffee shop, in conversations with coworkers, or by simply turning on the TV and watching people there. I call it the warm and cold game.

**This is how it works:** Instead of listening to a person's story, listen to her aliveness. When someone talks, pay attention to whether her energy level increases (warmer) or decreases (colder).

That's all you have to do at this point. Just observe, pay attention, read people's energetic responses, and have fun with it. Later, we will take it a step further to where you observe someone's impact on you, how they inspire you—or not.

**One more thing:** While observing someone, notice the instances you get lost. These are the moments when you forget to pay attention, when you get pulled into the story, and when your mind starts to engage; you agree or disagree, you add your own opinions, or maybe you stop listening and get caught in your own thoughts. For now, just notice when this happens.

What you are learning is a new way of listening, an increased sensory awareness of what is going on around you.

## Your Aliveness Defined

Your aliveness is the amount of excitement, enthusiasm, energy, and life force you experience at any given moment. While little kids have lots of it, many adults have lost some of their natural zest for life. Try to keep up with a group of six to nine year olds, and you will know what I mean.

I decided to put this to the test one summer day when I was about 16 years old and followed my three little cousins around . . . just for kicks and to see what life was like for a little boy in the summertime in Chile. I was beat after only a few hours. Climbing the mountains behind our cabin and sliding down the dry pine needles on self-constructed toboggans, running around in the woods playing fantasy bad-guy / good-guy games, venturing down the big ravine to the beach, jumping over tree branches and climbing every obstacle had more than done it for me. Not so the boys. While I went home to take a well-earned break, they were on their way to other adventures.

By listening to aliveness—instead of listening to thoughts and words—you start to perceive the world for what it really is. People become who they truly are, through the magic of your attention. As you see the world, it becomes.

Through the tool of observation, you learn to see past the mask someone puts up or the picture you've already made of them; you look through the pretense and see the person who's really there. This is complex, as your mind wants to constantly come up with an answer or get to a conclusion. Be okay with not having an answer and not having an opinion right away about someone or a situation.

With practice, you become more silent inside and enter a state of contemplation in which you become less distracted by the outside world. You see things with more accuracy and clarity.

By listening to aliveness, you see to the root cause of each situation. By quietly observing yourself and others, you become aware of each person's true intelligence and unique essence. It creates a feeling of deep love and happiness.

NOTE

Distinguishing between thoughts and sensory impulses takes practice. Your thoughts tell you what you think you want—which might be true or not—while your sensory impulses provide you with a more accurate reading of your real needs. Maybe you had a fight with your spouse, for example, and your mind is telling you to quit. It is reasoning that you had too many fights such as this, and that is time to leave your partner for good.

Reading your inner senses, you get a different story. Looking past your hurt and anger, you notice that the thought of leaving makes you deeply sad and that despite the fight you still love your spouse. This insight gives you the power to make a more mature and authentic decision about the future of your relationship. Instead of leaving, you decide to learn how to communicate better and find ways to make your own needs a priority.

If you have a difficult time accurately reading aliveness, relax. We will revisit this principle several times throughout the book and introduce diverse ways of integrating it into your life. In the process, you will paint a vision for your life, based on the elements (activities, places, people, and instances) that inspire you.

# Step Two: Gain Clarity

**Transformation Tools**

- **Open-Ended Questions**

- **Differentiation**

Now that you have found out how to enhance your body awareness by observing what increases your energy, let's take it a step further. Now, you get a chance to take your discoveries and deepen them by adding more color, more depth, and more detail to what makes you happy.

You will do this by distinguishing change patterns in your life. This will help you to understand which activities bring you alive and which ones don't. By observing how your environment and the people around you change at any given moment, you gain clarity about how even the smallest details affect you. Understanding what puts you at ease adds more balance to your life and brings you closer to your heart's calling.

HOW IT WORKS

Let's say that in Step One you realized that you love taking pictures. In Step Two, you want to be more specific and find out exactly how this works best for you. To do this, use the tool of asking open-ended questions:

Where do you like taking pictures? What's your preference as to the location? What about taking pictures makes you happy? When do you like taking pictures? What do you like to photograph? Which subjects inspire you more than others?

To find the answers, use the tool of observation you learned in Step One, and observe how your energy level goes up—or down—with each question and with each answer.

Do you have more fun taking pictures of children, adults, nature, or animals? Do you prefer working in a studio with backdrops, lights, and props or in nature? What do you love doing most with your finished work? Do you enjoy manipulating your images and creating works of art on your computer? Do you like turning them into cards and give them away to friends and family? Do you get excited about the idea of printing them and turning them into framed photographs? Would you like to sell them, give them away, or collect them for yourself?

By making specific distinctions, you gain clarity about the elements in your life that make you happy. Often you will observe a sense of relaxation and ease when you engage in something you love. Use observation to notice what lights you up and the tool of differentiation to identify every energetic detail that adds to your life and environment.

*The second step on your path takes you to the center of your being.*

By being as specific as you can about what it is that you love doing, you discover your personal identity and motivation in life.

Many people like to take pictures. By recognizing what it is about photography that makes you happy, you can set yourself apart from other people with the same interest. By fine-tuning your passion down to the most miniscule detail, you are able to experience more joy and excitement with everything you do.

My daughter loves to garden. Whenever she is in a bad mood, she just has to step outside, weed a little or water her plants and her mood improves. It works every time. When I asked her what it is about gardening that makes her happy, she responded, "Oh, I don't know, it relaxes me, and I like to take care of things and see them grow." This answer fits perfectly with her nature. Ever since she was a little girl, she cared about plants, people, and animals. She has a deep interest in nurturing things and making them feel better.

I like gardening too, yet for me the motivation is different. I like to make things beautiful and while I like to nurture and see things grow, my gardening is inspired by a need for order and beauty. That need shows up in just about everything I do.

*By narrowing things down to their essence, you will get to the core motivation of your life.*

Let me demonstrate this with yet another example: Let's say that in Step One you discovered that you love writing and journaling. In Step Two, you explore this newfound passion a bit closer and ask some open-ended questions: When and where do you have the most fun writing? What times of the day are best for it? Does it matter whether you write in the morning or in the evening? Is the result the same or different? What do you most enjoy writing about?

By answering these questions, you realize that you love going to a coffee shop for your daily journaling. The smell of fresh ground coffee, the background noise of people laughing, placing their orders, and talking to friends makes you feel protected and calm. It inspires you, and your writing becomes more playful and creative.

Next, you can get even more specific about your coffee-house writing experience by exploring whether you enjoy all coffee houses the same or if some are more soothing than others and why? How about time of day? Do you enjoy the morning rush, or do you prefer writing in the afternoon when things calm down a little?

By being this detailed, you fine-tune your experiences and gain clarity about the elements, the places, the situations, and the people in your life that add to your energy and aliveness.

In the process, your life will gain depth, clarity, and joy. Your timing will improve and your life will flow with more ease and pleasure. By distinguishing what turns you on in all areas of life, you tap into the core wisdom of your being.

Asking open-ended questions and differentiating between increased and decreased aliveness will help you to make this step highly effective.

**How to make effective distinctions:** To become proficient at using the tool of differentiation, start noticing the changes that are happening in your environment.

At first, you will notice obvious differences; for example the light or the temperature in a room going up or down. With practice, you become more attuned to what's going on around you at any given moment. Use open-ended questions to make accurate comparisons and ask yourself whether things are the same or different. Is your level of attention the same or has it changed from the previous chapter? Is the mood in your office the same, or is it different from when you arrived? Are you as happy or as nervous as you were an hour ago?

Once you master making these simple distinctions in your environment, start noticing change patterns in your own system. For example, you might feel nervous before making an important phone call. How do you feel after the call is completed? Is your energy the same or different from before? Be careful not to interpret your changes. We only want to notice specific differences and not evaluate or judge the outcome.

Another way of practicing the tool of differentiation is by observing physical changes in your body. To do this, get in front of a mirror and study your face. Did you ever notice that the two sides of your face are not identical? To become aware of how different they are, cover the right side of your face with your right hand and study your left side. Keep your nose uncovered. Observe carefully. What do you see on this side of your face? Is it relaxed, tense, open, tired, or awake?

Now, take your right hand down and cover the left side of your face with your left hand. Again, keep your nose uncovered. What do you see on this side of your face? Is it the same or different from your left side? Does the eye have the same expression? Is it more relaxed or tenser? Is the shape of your mouth the same or different from the way it looked on the left side?

Notice the smallest differences without judgment or opinion.

Now, look at your full face. What do you see now? Can you still identify the different sides? Ask yourself, if you didn't know the person looking at you in the mirror, what is her facial expression? What does this face tell you without using words? What is the overall communication?

For detailed instructions on this step, go to "Self-Awareness Exercise: What Your Face Reveals about You" at the end of this chapter.

Here is another way to practice this tool. Go to a window and look outside. Now cover one eye and observe the view out of your uncovered eye. Notice the colors, the depth of what you see, the mood of the environment, etc. Uncover your eye and cover the other one. Again, look out the window and take in the view. Do things look the same or different looking out of this eye? If you see a difference, describe it.

To me, the world often looks more serious and less colorful looking out of my right eye. Out of my left eye, the colors are generally brighter and things seem more cheerful.

It is possible that you don't make any distinctions at first, and that is fine—just keep practicing. Maybe the two sides of your brain are balanced and you see the world the same out of both eyes. If you do see differences, which eye sees the world for what it is? In my case, is the world serious or cheerful? Which one of my eyes is right?

**Why is this important?** By noticing subtle changes in your environment and in yourself, you can respond to them accordingly. Just as you put on a sweater when the temperature in the room drops, you can respond to a change in energy by taking a walk, laying down for a nap, or making a cup of tea. This allows you to keep your balance and not exhaust yourself or be exhausted by others.

Discerning and responding to energy patterns, in your body and in your environment, allows you to keep your rhythm and stay balanced. Your timing improves, you experience a sense of flow, and your life becomes peaceful and calm. You gain confidence and become happier.

---

### Open-Ended Questions Defined

In contrast to close-ended questions, open-ended questions cannot be answered with yes or no. They often begin with who, what, how, where, and when. They stir enthusiasm and energy in the respondent.

Open-ended questions elicit curiosity and help people to be more creative and imaginative when responding.

To help you jump-start the process of inquiry, look at the list of open-ended questions in the appendix section of this book. You can use them as an inspiration until you find the questions that best fit you.

---

# Step Three: Make Adjustments

## Transformation Tools

- **Feedback**

- **Boldness**

As we have seen in the previous sections, the language of your soul is energetic. It speaks through your aliveness. The things that light you up resonate with your whole being: body, mind, and soul. They make you stronger. You want them in your life. The things that don't bring you alive will make you weaker. Start to eliminate them one by one.

The main characteristic of this part of your journey is an increased level of energy, which leads to more optimism. By paying attention to your aliveness and the impact your surroundings have on you, you begin to better understand your true character. This gives you confidence and increased self-esteem. You feel younger and more mature. Things start to flow with ease and the perception of yourself and your environment becomes increasingly accurate.

The confidence you gained in Step One and Step Two gives you the courage to ask for the things you want and to follow your path.

*On the third step of your path it's time to be bold.*

By adding more of what makes you happy and by eliminating the things that bring you down, you can start to organize your life around your energetic responses.

While this is a fairly simple and straightforward principle, it takes courage and awareness to apply it; courage to eliminate from your life what doesn't serve you and clarity to make the decisions that expand your life and make it magical.

After her summer break, my daughter told me that she didn't want to go back to school. Wow, imagine if you decided not to go back to work after your vacation. The announcement was all the more surprising as my daughter had always been quite successful at school. She's had the best teachers, great friends, and amazing challenges; she had skipped a grade and is smart as a whip. And now she was telling me that she didn't want to go back.

Looking at it, I had to admit that she hadn't been as happy as she used to be (distinction). And while I noticed the change in her (observation), I had convinced myself that all she needed was a well-deserved summer break and that things would go back to normal in the fall (denial). Yet, she was making her case with great determination, and her father and I decided to help her make a change.

We found out that our school district provides a well established homeschooling program, including a private teacher free of charge with classes twice a week. This would give her the challenges she loved and was missing: setting her own schedule, delving into fields that interest her, taking on responsibility for her own learning, etc.

Once the decision was made to homeschool her for one year, everything changed. Her depressed, sad attitude vanished and her beautiful self once again emerged — happy, relaxed, lit up, and full of self-esteem (observation and differentiation). This was my daughter making her own luck, standing up for herself and saying, "I don't want to go back to school. It's not making me happy. It's not what I need."

In order to make useful adjustments, you have to be clear about what puts you at ease versus what adds pressure to your life. From the exercises and action steps in the previous chapter, you should have a good idea what those elements are.

If not, take time out to explore and reflect on your life. Discern what activities, people, experiences, and places add to or take away from your energy and pleasure. Make lists, create a vision board or make collages. Hire a coach and get feedback from friends. In

Chapter 6, "First Steps on Your Path," we delve into this part of your journey in more detail.

Once your foundation is strong, it's time to add another layer to the process. At this point, having clarity is not enough. Now, you need to be bold and take the steps that clear your life of negativity and happiness killers.

The tool to use here is feedback. Feedback will give you the information you need to make adjustments in your thoughts, your behavior, and your communication. It will provide you with the necessary details to make changes and adapt.

Accurate feedback gives you clarity, power, and puts the juice back into your life.

**How feedback works:** Pure feedback is simply saying what you see—in your own or someone else's actions or behavior—without giving your opinion. It is something you see that other people can also see.

With pure feedback, you should always light up. If you don't get brighter, more curious, and more alive, then you did not use feedback, but rather criticism, blaming, a projection, an opinion, or an accusation.

*Feedback offers no judgment. It does not make you wrong. It should never hurt.*

Using clear feedback, devoid of judgment and criticism, will allow you to make the adjustments that add to your happiness and well-being.

In Step Two, you asked yourself whether things were the same or different. Now it is time to find out what works and what doesn't work in your life. This simple inquiry will take any type of blame and judgment out of the process of making adjustments. It's not about whether you like or dislike a person or an activity. It's about what works or doesn't work and whether it is bringing you alive or not.

## Three Rules of Feedback

1. **What do you see that other people can also see?** Feedback is a way to share observable, measurable, and obvious information. If we can all see it, then it qualifies as feedback.

2. **Feedback is upbeat and positive.** Give feedback in a positive tone of voice, so that people feel your friendly intent behind it. Otherwise, it might come across as criticism and start an argument, even a nonverbal argument.

3. **Feedback is not the truth. It is what you see.** When you learn to give feedback, you can stop giving people your opinions.

For example, telling someone he sucks is a judgment; telling him that showing up late to every meeting doesn't work is giving feedback. Hating your job is a judgment. Realizing that your commute is long and that you get to work feeling depleted is feedback.

Next, use the tool of boldness to get rid of—or replace—the elements that bring you down. For example, you have a friend who keeps being mean to you. Every time you go out with her, she ignores you, puts you down, and makes you otherwise feel bad about yourself. She stands you up, is late for your appointments, and rarely keeps her word. She expects you to be there when she is in a pickle, but you stopped expecting her to return the favor.

Sounds bad, yes? This would never happen to you, no? You would be surprised how many people are in situations such as these. And, it's up to you to change it, set boundaries, and if things don't look up, end the friendship.

Sounds drastic? If you want to have a great life, you have to be ruthless about your happiness.

Let's use another example. A few months ago, you moved into an apartment because it was affordable and you were tired of looking. You had seen a few places you liked better, but they were much more expensive and this seemed like a safe choice. Now you notice that every time you come home your mood drops. The place is dark and the nearby street is loud. You tried to make it homier with bright curtains and scented candles, which helped a little.

Your brain keeps telling you that it's not that bad and that you are not home that much anyway. However, your heart is telling you another story. You don't feel happy here and the only way to change it is to move to a friendlier place.

What about activities, people, and circumstances that you cannot or simply will not eliminate? I recommend thinking of creative ways to transform any negative elements in your life into positive ones. For example, you think exercise is important and while you don't enjoy going to the gym, you force yourself to do it anyway. Because you don't want to give up fitness, think of alternative ways to make your exercise experience more fun. Maybe the gym isn't for you and you would rather workout in nature or at home? You also realize that you enjoy group activities and that joining a hiking group or a beach volleyball team on Sunday mornings would be a much better option to get in shape.

Or, let's say you feel obligated to call your mom every week, however, most of your phone conversations turn into complaints about her neighbors, her bad health, and your dad. Every time you get off the phone, you feel drained and irritated. This not only impacts your own mood but also that of your kids and your partner.

How could you change your interactions with your mother and make them more pleasant? First, find out what exactly it is that drains you throughout your conversations and change the topic to something more positive and uplifting. If that doesn't help, use feedback to make a change. Tell your mom that every time she complains about your dad it makes you sad (upset, tired, etc.). Tell her that you'd like to change your conversations to something more positive. Remember to keep your feedback free of judgment and criticism. "You always complain about Dad," or "Why do you have to be so pessimistic?" will make her defensive and most likely turn into an argument. It doesn't offer a solution for change.

You can have whatever you want and need to be happy. If at the moment this is hard for you to believe or accept, that's all right. For now, find someone—a partner or a friend—who shows you a more positive way of being and who reminds you that everything is possible.

# Self-Awareness Exercise—
# What Your Face Reveals about You

This exercise is designed to show you how your body metabolizes emotions. Not only do we process the food we eat, we also digest our emotions. If you experience anger for days, weeks, or even months, the impact of that anger will start to show in your body, especially in your face. I never forget how one morning, months after my divorce, I looked in the mirror and for some reason that instant I really saw myself: the disappointment and frustration of that time was clearly written on my face. You might have experienced this at certain times yourself. The good news is that it goes both ways. When you are happy and satisfied with your life, your face shows it as well.

To practice reading visual clues on a face, look at the following pictures of five different people. Look at the faces and observe what you see. What are the expressions on each face? How are they different? What emotions do you see?

To help you, I have added a list of possible emotions at the end of this section. If you prefer, come up with your own. Be as objective as you can and avoid making interpretations.

**Picture 1**

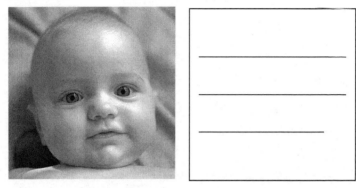

What do you see in this baby's face? Use the box to record your observations.

*For example: I see bright eyes, joy, a high forehead, a balanced face, beauty, a sense of wonder in the gaze, curiosity, trust, one eyebrow is a bit more pronounced than the other, softness.*

**Picture 2**

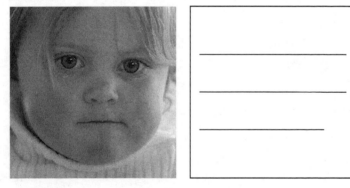

*In the toddler's face I see blushed cheeks, a colored chin, clear eyes, and a tight mouth. There is a look of determination on her face.*

**Picture 3**

*The man's face isn't balanced. His right eye is more open than his left and it sits higher. He has lines on his forehead, he looks straight at the camera, and his overall expression is determined and friendly.*

What do you observe? Use the box to record your observations.

**Picture 4**

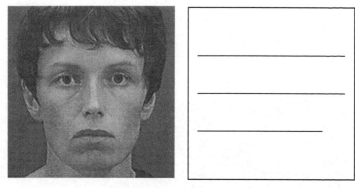

*I observe lifeless eyes, a downturned mouth, and tension in the jaw. There is a narrow pinched quality to the face. The right eye is more closed than the left eye is. The overall expression is one of anger and resignation.*

Take a few moments for this exercise. It is important to sharpen your awareness so you can have a deeper understanding of yourself and the people around you.

This is how you observe and make distinctions, the first step in transforming yourself.

**Picture 5**

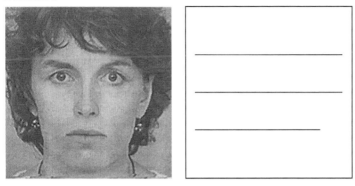

*Here, I see curiosity and aliveness. The two eyes are bright, the right eye is slightly smaller than the left one and both eyes look straight at me. Her mouth is relaxed with a full lower lip.*

Now it's your turn. If you feel courageous, step in front of a mirror, relax your face and observe your own expression. What do you see in your face?

## Your Picture

Your Picture Goes Here

## Your Observations

**Observation Clues and Emotions You Might Be Able to See:**

| | | |
|---|---|---|
| Anger | Balance | Beauty |
| Curiosity | Boredom | Depression |
| Determination | Direct | Distant |
| Disappointment | Disinterest | Dissatisfaction |
| Enthusiasm | Excitement | Fear |
| Frustration | Happiness | Hesitation |
| Joy | Playfulness | Pleasure |
| Sadness | Serenity | Softness |
| Tiredness | Trust | Wonder |

*Mantra*—Throughout the day, follow this simple strategy: realize when your energy is up and when your energy is down. This helps you to integrate and practice the six fundamental transformation tools we introduced in this chapter: *observation* (pay attention to your energy), *curiosity* (stay open and don't assume the answer), *open-ended questions* (what brings your energy up and what brings it down?), *differentiation* (is your energy the same or different throughout the day?), *feedback* (give yourself clear feedback on what's happening), and *boldness* (have the courage to try a new approach).

# CHAPTER 4
# Obstacles on Your Way

As with any journey, there will be obstacles and before we move on to Chapter 5, "Transformation in Action," let's address the ones that will most likely interfere with your process of self-discovery.

## Your Rational Mind

*The intuitive mind is a sacred gift and the rational mind is a faithful servant. We have created a society that honors the servant and has forgotten the gift.*

—**Albert Einstein,** German physicist

While reading the various chapters and doing some of the exercises, are you aware of how your mind is trying to interfere? Is it telling you that it can't be this easy, that life isn't just about doing what is fun or what you enjoy?

Is it arguing that if everybody only did what he or she wanted, the world would soon end in chaos, and so on and so forth?

That voice in your head is the reason it's so hard to find your gifts in the first place. It will *constantly* try to interfere with your happiness. And what's more, most times you won't even notice. Because by this point, it has become second nature to be in your head instead of in the present; it's what you have practiced your whole life.

The biggest challenge in listening to your soul isn't finding out what it is you love doing or what brings you joy. The biggest challenge in following your heart is to stop listening to your mind. By learning how to read aliveness, you are able to understand your mind as well as your heart—and the voice of fear that's so persuasive. Becoming efficient at distinguishing between your head and your heart will take practice and constant vigilance, because your head will try to interfere at every turn in the road.

Let's not discredit your thinking machine. It is an important tool in your toolbox and when used properly, it is highly effective. However, it has its limitation and, much like a railroad track, the path is fixed in place. It does not have the freedom to fly like a plane or float like a balloon. If you are stuck with only rational thought, life becomes repetitive and stale. You think what you've thought before, pick up opinions from the people around you, and copy what others have done without room for innovation or intuition. Taken to the extreme, you become robotic.

There are instances when rational thought is important. For our purpose, however, we want to leave the stable tracks of logic behind and venture into the world of creativity, energy, and intuition. By quieting your mind and diverting your attention away from your thoughts, by listening to aliveness and paying attention to the responses of your body, you will expand your awareness and enter the realm of unlimited possibilities. You experience greater freedom, more depth, increased awareness and get face to face with reality. Reality transcends logic and by going beyond thought, you have access to creativity and infinite possibilities.

When your rational mind is quiet, you are fully present and can glimpse reality for what it really is; that's when you notice the beautiful sunset, the kindness on your friend's faces, the joy in a kid's voice, the love in your partner's eyes, and the vibrant colors around you. You feel peaceful and full of joy and deeply connected to the world and everything in it.

# The Voice of Fear

*Life expands in direct proportion to one's courage.*

—**Anaïs Nin,** French author

Fear shows up in different forms. The physical sensation of it is easy to recognize: shaky legs when you are standing at the edge of a cliff and sweaty hands before delivering an important speech.

Yet, there is a more subtle form of fear, a voice in your head, a story that you are telling yourself, which is much harder to identify.

Typically, fear doesn't just say, "I am scared"; that would be too easy. More likely, it will appear in the form of a story—one that soothes you and makes you feel comfortable. The voice that tries to convince you that moving forward and facing important changes is really not that important right now.

Wherever your biggest fear is hidden, it's often the source of your biggest desire. Whenever someone tells me what they don't want to do (I really don't like getting up in front of people, I am not a good singer, I am a really quiet person, etc.), I dare them to do that exact thing. Sure enough, when they talk about the topic, it's often where they get most excited.

Here are some of the voices of fear:

## Fear in Business

- It has to be perfect before I can put it out in the marketplace.

- I don't like my job but it's better than not having one.

- I have to have a really good business plan before I can start my own venture.

- Somebody much smarter than me should do this.

- Good clients are hard to find.

- Money really is not that important to me.

- I am not sure that I can do this.

- I don't deserve it.

- I need a partner if I really want to be successful.

- Who am I to have a big business?

- My job is not that challenging anymore but I like the regular paycheck.

- I cannot sell.

- Nobody will buy from me.

## Fear in Relationships

- It's hard to find a good man / woman.

- The only thing women are interested in is money.

- The only thing men want is sex.

- First, I have to lose weight and then I can have a relationship.

- I don't think the right person is out there for me.

- If I ask for what I want in my relationship, it will fall apart.

- It's not worth the trouble. Having kids is too much work.

- If I end this relationship, I might never find a good partner again.

- I am not good looking enough to deserve a great man / woman.

- I don't want to get hurt again.

## Fear in Life

- I don't have many friends and that's okay.

- I don't want to stir up any trouble.

- I can't afford it.

- If I don't do what others expect of me, I end up all alone.

- My life is nice and quiet.

- I think my life will be much easier once I . . .

- If I say what I really think, nobody will like me.

- I am not good enough.

- I am not worthy.

- People don't really like me.

## Coming to Conclusions

Listening to someone's aliveness requires you to stay alert and not to come to any conclusions. Every time you think you know the answer to something or to someone's problem, you are in danger of making up a fictitious scenario. Remind yourself to stay objective and to be okay with not knowing.

This might be uncomfortable at first (we want to have an answer for everything), yet not drawing conclusions has enormous power because it removes your rational thought from the equation. You don't have to be an expert or have all of the answers. You don't have to tell anybody, especially not yourself, what to do and who to be.

**How to use observation instead of conclusions:** Did you ever share an incident with someone just to have him interrupt you halfway through your story to tell you what he thought you should have done? Most likely, he jumped to conclusions and, without having all the facts, made up his own version of the facts—which might or might not have had anything to do with what you meant to say.

Had he taken the time to let you finish, observing you and listening to your truth (instead of his), the experience would have been a different one. You would have felt understood and appreciated. As it was, you felt misunderstood and let down.

- Observations are open, questioning, and inconclusive.

- Conclusions create the illusion of an answer and inhibit your ability to observe.

# Making Interpretations

We interpret when we add meaning to something without having the facts. Be aware of this trap. Interpretations are misleading; they cloud your perception of reality.

For example, you watch a teenager sitting curbside at the entrance of a school waiting to be picked up. It is long after school has gotten out and your mind tells you that his parents are irresponsible. Bam, you made an interpretation. You make up a story from watching a kid sitting outside the school entrance without having the facts about what's really going on.

Your story might be correct, but there are also many other scenarios that could explain why the teenager is sitting there: he got out early from an after-school program. He has already been home and is now meeting some friends in front of the school. He lives in walking distance but doesn't want to go home. And so on. Until you ask the kid, you won't know which, if any, of these stories is correct. You simply have the (unconscious) habit of assuming that you have the right one.

Let's take two of the pictures from our Self Awareness Exercise as another example. Instead of observing a face, most people interpret it and add meaning to what they see.

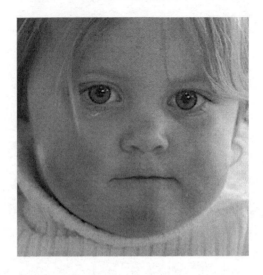

By observing this girl's face, you notice that one of her eyes sits a bit lower than the other one, that her mouth is shut tight, that her cheeks are colored and her eyes are bright.

If you observe that she is embarrassed because her face is blushed, you are making an interpretation. Thinking that she is tense about something, because her mouth is tight, is another interpretation.

Do you see the difference? You can't know whether she is embarrassed or tense. You are making this up. To someone else, her red cheeks mean that she has a fever and to yet another person her flushed face is a sign that she is excited about something.

Why is this important? By making up stories and interpreting the world around you, you can't see it for what it really is. Your perception is warped. You have created a contrived and mostly negative interpretation of what's really going on.

Let's view another picture.

In this man's face, one eye is a bit smaller than the other one and it sits a little lower. There is a line between his eyebrows, several lines on his forehead, his mouth is straight, and he looks directly at you.

To observe that the man is untrusting and hiding something because his facial muscles are tense, is an interpretation. It's not something you can know.

Be attentive and aware of how your mind works. It will tell you thoughts all the time that cloud your perception of what's really going on. A slow driver in front of you? Idiot! A beautiful woman at the side of a handsome man? Lucky couple. Whatever your mind tells you might or might not be the truth. The only thing you know for sure is what you see. Everything else is made up.

## Outside Influences

While most obstacles arise from your own habits and thinking patterns, you might also encounter a few hurdles from the outside world, particularly from your family, colleagues, and close friends.

When I decided to leave Germany and move to the United States, some of my best friends became very angry. "What are you thinking?" they asked, "You can't just take your kids and move to a foreign country." "How are you going to make a living?" "What about your family?" "What if you don't make it?"

There were only a few who encouraged me and even fewer asked me if I needed any help.

*Be prepared.* When you change, the world around you often decides to resist your forward motion. Your family might think you are crazy (mine did), your friends might feel abandoned, and your spouse could try to stop you. What you are confronted with at this point is not your own fear, but other people's fears, doubts, and worries.

If the people around you realize that what's really bothering them in the face of your transformation is their own need for growth and expansion, this can turn into an opportunity for everyone.

**My tip:** don't burn your bridges. Have compassion for the people you care about, while at the same time staying strong and moving toward your goal.

These are a few of the obstacles you encounter on your path of self-discovery. Knowing and recognizing them is a crucial part of moving forward. If, in addition, you learn to accept those obstacles for what they are, just roadblocks on your journey and not the truth, your transformation process will accelerate.

*Mantra*—Don't be afraid to make mistakes. Obstacles are an integral part of any journey, so embrace them wholeheartedly. Once you step into your fears, you might discover that what lives on the other side is pure excitement and enthusiasm.

# CHAPTER 5
## Transformation in Action

In Chapter 3, "Read Your Identity Blueprint," I provided you with clearly defined steps to help you discover your passion and personal calling. These steps are tried and proven; they will expand the way you see yourself and help you to understand your life and mission.

In this chapter, you practice the tools and integrate them so they become second nature. You internalize the transformation process and learn to maintain a level of happiness that you thought impossible.

If you put in the time to review and practice what you have learned, you create a level of attraction that makes your life irresistible. To see the results you desire, you have to keep polishing your skills. I can't stress this enough: it requires vigilance, honesty, and discipline to live your destiny and to create a life that is fulfilling.

# What Lights You Up?

*If you shine your light, others can do the same. You can ignite a chain reaction of illumination that is unstoppable.*

—**Dylan Patterson**, photographer

In the previous chapter, I showed you how to read and listen to aliveness. Now, it's time to apply it to your life. For the next few days and weeks observe the activities, the places, the instances, and the people who inspire you and make you happy. Record them in a notebook.

Consciously and intentionally, use this as a time of exploration. Take as long as you need to find out what sets your heart on fire. This is a special process that can't be rushed; your senses, your spirit, and your soul are awakening. Be gentle with yourself and allow time to wonder, to question, and be all right with not having any answers at this point. You will want to jump into action and make things happen. Now is not that time, but it is coming soon.

How long this process of exploration takes is entirely up to you. Be respectful of your own needs and avoid falling into the trap of forcing an outcome. You will know when the time is right to move on. Trust that your natural desire to find out what's next on your path will emerge and that life (and the universe) will guide you from step to step.

When my youngest daughter was in first grade, she had the hardest time learning how to read. It was almost as if her brain was refusing to get it. I remember our walls being plastered with signs: hat, cat, map, nap, clap. While I was freaking out (a little), my daughter was completely unscathed.

When second grade came around, it all of a sudden clicked and she was ready to read: slowly at first, but then faster and faster. Soon she was reading far above her grade level; she devoured book after book and received the highest marks in her reading program. I remember one summer she read close to 50 books. Then she skipped fourth grade and just kept going.

So, if you don't know what you want to do and what you are good at, don't worry. It will show up when you are ready.

When I was at that point in my own life, I carried a notebook around in my purse at all times. I recorded anything and everything that made me curious and turned me on—from shoes I saw in a window display, haircuts I thought looked cute, places I wanted to live in, quotes and phrases that inspired me, photographs I loved, plates that I'd like to eat from, furniture to put in my apartment, beautiful people that I wanted to meet, etc.

It was like going on a treasure hunt for the things that brought me pleasure and joy. Still to this day, that's how I feel about my profession of working with people and helping them find their true identities. It's like digging for jewels and finding hidden treasures.

## ACTION STEP

**The Puzzle Exercise**

Take a piece of paper and draw a blank puzzle. To make this easy for you, I created a *blank puzzle template* that you can find in the Appendix. Imagine that each puzzle piece represents an area of your life that inspires you.

For example, let's say you are interested in photography and like taking pictures wherever you go. Every time you do this, you feel good about yourself, your energy increases, you get happier, and you feel inspired. This is one of the pieces of your puzzle and you write photography or taking pictures on one of the blank puzzle pieces.

Next, let's imagine you also enjoy hiking and love being in nature. These two activities also become puzzle pieces. Keep filling in the blank pieces whenever you notice an activity that lights you up, something you enjoy doing that makes you forget time. This can be anything—traveling, dancing, cooking, entertaining, hiking, painting, etc.

To qualify to be a puzzle piece, the activity has to significantly increase your level of aliveness every time you do it—for an extended period of time (several hours). Be aware of this. We all have talents that don't keep us engaged for long periods of time. I am really good at organizing, for example, but after an hour of rearranging my bookshelf or linen closet, I feel exhausted and drained. Just because you are good at something doesn't mean it is your passion.

Once you identify your puzzle pieces, sort them into groups, such as projects, business ideas, your ideal lifestyle, etc. We will expand on this in Chapter 7, "Design the Dream." All the pieces are based on what you love, so the activities will be naturally fun and enjoyable, and create fulfilling experiences.

By getting clear about what lights you up, you can start filling in the pieces of the vision for your life.

# Put Energy First

*When you find your path, you must not be afraid. You need to have sufficient courage to make mistakes.*

—**Paulo Coelho**, *Brida*

If you want to be a more vibrant and authentic version of yourself, you have to unlearn much of what you know and hold dear. You have to embrace uncertainty, learn to be uncomfortable, get use to fear and start looking at your life in an expanded and more conscious way.

As you learned in Chapter 3, "Read Your Identity Blueprint," the first step on your path is to get out of your head and into your body.

This means to stop listening to your fears and worries and instead start reading the subtle clues of your vibrations and sensations; to tune into the voice of your soul by paying attention to your aliveness, your mojo; to find out what truly lights your fire and inspires you.

The questions you ask yourself at this point are, "What do I want?" "What makes me happy?" and "How do I get there?" If it seems hard to find those answers right now, that's okay. Let me assure you that the only person who knows them is you and that you can find them. It is a matter of reading the signs correctly that will lead you to your core truth.

Pay attention to your vibrations, the magnetic resonance you have with people, situations, places, and activities. Notice what inspires you, the joy you bring to a conversation, the energy you get from playing an instrument, or the enthusiasm you experience when performing a specific task.

When my son was little, he took enormous pleasure in organizing the world around him. I remember him arranging magazine and flyer racks outside our local Whole Foods, singing and completely immersed in the task.

In your heart, you know what you need to be happy; the answers are written into every fiber of your being. What's holding you back is your brain, because that's where you go for answers most of the time. So, when I ask you what it is you want, you go and check in with your head, and guess what you find there? Old answers and recycled ideas that will keep you hooked in the same traps everyone else falls into.

Instead of trusting yourself, you listen to fear; instead of making joy the measurement of your life, you think that the money in your bank account and your degrees and titles will be the scale of how well you are doing. You believe that winning is everything and being vulnerable is a sign of weakness, so you put up a strong façade and ignore your deepest needs.

You stick with what's safe, a job, for example, that doesn't make you happy because you are afraid of the judgment of others. You compromise your happiness for fear of losing the person you love. You keep quiet when what you really want is to speak up.

Fear of failure, fear of looking bad, fear of getting hurt, fear of being left behind, fear of losing love, or fear of making a fool of yourself are the main reasons people stay trapped in jobs and lives they don't love. In Chapter 4, "Obstacles on Your Way," I gave you a list of the different kinds of fears, how to distinguish them, and how to avoid believing them.

One way to escape the common trap of fear is by paying attention to your body sensations—the joy that arises when you play the piano, the excitement you feel when you step on a stage to make a presentation— instead of listening to your mind telling you that being on stage is scary.

In his fabulous book, *The Book of Secrets*, Deepak Chopra describes how every single cell of your body knows exactly what you are born to do. And, to the extent you deviate from your soul's purpose, your body gets tired, angry, sad, and ultimately sick.

By putting energy first, you learn to read your tension and relaxation patterns and understand how your body responds to stress and to pleasure. Putting energy first means to follow your mojo by making happiness a priority in your life.

# Ask for Feedback

A brave way to find out more about your unique talents is to ask others for feedback.

Ask them: "What do you see in me?" "What special qualities about me do you cherish?" "What am I adding to your life?"

As I mentioned in Chapter 1, "The Three Secrets," part of the reason you can't see your own brilliance is that for you it is completely normal. You are being you every day and can't see the impact you have on the world. By asking others for feedback, you have an opportunity to perceive yourself through their eyes.

When you do this, it's important to listen and be grateful for the feedback you receive. Have you ever noticed the tendency to downplay the praise we get from others? When you ask for feedback, make sure you gracefully respect and accept it. Never argue with something you are being acknowledged for. Thank the person who provides the insight and express your appreciation for her contribution.

IMPORTANT

Only ask people for feedback who have your best interest at heart—lest you solicit negative feedback or criticism, which is rather destructive.

ACTION STEP

Make a list of 10 people and ask each one of them these specific questions:

- What do you see are my strengths?

- What issues would you trust me with?

- How have I contributed to your life?

- What are my unique qualities that set me apart from others?

- What are my talents?

Record the answers you receive and evaluate them. Did people tell you the same thing about your talents and qualities? What did they point out about you? How do they think you are special?

Looking at your notes, what patterns can you detect? What one thing stands out? One consistent piece of feedback I get from people is that I am easy to talk to. Even when I was as young as nine years old, a friend told me that it was fun to talk to me. It is something that I have heard my whole life.

What is that for you? The answers will reveal part of your inner essence.

# Self-Awareness Exercise— Rate Your Level of Aliveness

This exercise is designed to give you a better understanding of what's going on in your body at any given moment. It will help you to become more aware of your inner sensory system. There is a direct connection between what you feel and what you think, but sometimes what you think is not what's really going on. We often react to sensations in our body by making up a story as to what the sensations mean. With increased awareness and a better understanding of your feelings, you start to see things for what they are—and not for what you think they are.

Let me give you an example. I was traveling to Europe, working on my computer on the plane and having a good time. All of a sudden, I felt sad. Was I really a good mom, traveling this much? Shouldn't I be home more? I was sure my daughter missed me.

These were the thoughts going through my mind. "Wait a minute," I thought, "What is really going on here?" A minute ago, I had been perfectly content, working on my current project, and all of a sudden I was wondering whether I was a good mom? I knew my daughter was perfectly well taken care of when I was gone and that in a few days I would be back home.

I am very sensitive to what's going in my environment, so I looked up and noticed that the person next to me was watching a movie, which had turned quite sad. I had picked up on her mood and my mind had added its own version as to why I was feeling sad.

Do you see what I mean? Feelings are contagious. It happens all the time: You are sitting in a coffeehouse working on your computer when all of a sudden you get angry. You might think it has to do with you, when it's possibly the person sitting next to you who is feeling upset.

**This Exercise Consists of Two Parts**
First, you will rate your level of happiness on a scale from 1 to 10. Then, you will learn to assess your current mood, your feelings, and aliveness.

To start, sit in a quiet place and close your eyes. Take a deep breath, relax, and tune into your body. On a scale from 1 to 10, where are you right now as far as your aliveness, your happiness, and your overall enthusiasm for life? Do you have a number? Write it in the box below:

My number:

Next, tune in again and describe what you are feeling in your body. Are you excited about something? Are you anxious to do this exercise correctly? Are you tired, distracted, or bored? Using the list of sensations, pick the ones that describe what you are feeling at this moment. You can pick as many as you want. If you don't find the word that describes your state of aliveness, feel free to come up with your own. The list is merely meant to serve as a starting point.

My sensation(s): 
```
[                              ]
```

## List of Sensations

| | | | |
|---|---|---|---|
| Angry | Anxious | Bored | Calm |
| Confident | Confused | Curious | Depressed |
| Disappointed | Encouraged | Enthusiastic | Excited |
| Frustrated | Grateful | Happy | Inspired |
| Joyful | Lonely | Nervous | Numb |
| Playful | Relaxed | Rested | Restless |
| Sad | Tense | Tired | Trusting |

Practice checking in with yourself throughout the day. If you want to do this exercise on a regular basis, you can use Worksheet 3 in the Appendix. I recommend you take a few minutes every day for a week or two to check in with yourself: How much aliveness do you feel on a scale from 1 to 10 in the mornings, at lunch, and in the evenings? What are the sensations that go along with it?

This exercise will help you to become more aware of your surroundings and the impact they have on you. You can find out if there are certain people, events, places, or situations that have a positive or negative effect on you. You become more attuned to what brings your energy up and what turns you off.

These are important steps in finding out what brings you alive, which in turn will lead you to your gifts and passions.

*Mantra*—Now is the time to explore. Your mantra at this point is: "Everything is possible." Use the tool of curiosity to keep an open mind. Be honest with yourself and invite exciting new ideas and experiences. Whenever fear (doubt, hesitation, worry, or disbelief) starts to limit your perception of what you can do, have, and be, don't back away. Recognize the little voice in your head, accept it and learn to push into it by gently expanding beyond your fear, one step at a time.

# THE JOURNEY BEGINS

*Whenever we do something that fills us with enthusiasm, we are following our legend.*

—**Paulo Coelho**, *The Alchemist*

Like many epic journeys, we started yours by exploring what's possible. Now it is time to put the pieces together and use your imagination to venture into the unknown.

The great explorers of the world had a vague idea of where they were heading. What they didn't know was what to expect on their journey or at their destination. They had a goal to explore uncharted territory, but they were acutely aware of the fact that they were stepping into the unknown. It's what made their journeys electrifying and scary at the same time. That's what you want to embrace, a sense of nervous anticipation mixed with the curiosity that comes from leaving behind what you know.

This might challenge your beliefs. Stay open to not knowing. Let go of the idea you have of yourself and embrace the mystery called you. This will expand your perception of what's possible and make room for creating whom you are, where you want to go, and whom you want to be.

# CHAPTER 6
# First Steps on Your Path

In Chapter 1, I let you in on the three secrets that keep you from following your passion, and we looked at the instances in your life that got you where you are today. In Chapter 3, I gave you transformational tools to help you identify your life purpose.

In this chapter, I challenge you to let it all go; start with a clean slate, a blank canvas, and lots of colors to fill in your vision. Your state of mind is one of wonder and your mantra is "I don't know."

Enjoy.

# Look into the Mirror of Your Life

*We don't see things as they are,*
*we see them as we are.*

—**Anaïs Nin,** French author

It is difficult to see your life for what it really is. It's even harder to see yourself for who you really are. You can look in a mirror and see your image, your outside appearance. But how do you go deeper than that? How can you look right into your soul?

In previous chapters you learned how to connect with your soul by reading your sensory response system. You did exercises to find out what inspires you and makes you happy. Now, let's take it a step further and explore how the world and the people around you change with your presence. This will deepen your understanding of who you are and why you are here.

*To know your own beauty, you have to see how the world changes with you in it.*

Do you know what you are adding to the world and to the people around you? Are you aware of the unique flavor you bring to someone's life? Have you seen how a room changes when you enter it? Do you know the vibe you bring to a party?

Whatever you see in others is a part of you. The beauty and kindness you see in another person resonates with the beauty and kindness within you. The generosity you appreciate in another person stirs something that's true to you. By looking into the mirror of your life, you get glimpses of your own brilliance.

By observing the magnetic resonance you have with your environment, you become aware of your own qualities. You start to understand what it is that you add to a conversation, a room of people, or a friend's life.

It takes a keen eye to read the clues just right. It's like measuring the temperature around you. Are you inspiring people with your passion? Are you elevating the mood in a room? What is the impact you have on the world?

When I first paid attention to this, I realized that more often than not I was turning people off. There was a quality to my responses that shut them down. As a result, conversations stalled and people lost interest in the topic at hand. I was shocked, as I had never noticed this before. With this new insight, I began to change the way I interacted with others. For the first time, I became consciously interested in what brought someone alive and what didn't. It was a humbling and healing experience.

ACTION STEP

For one day, observe your environment and how it resonates with you. How are people responding to you? What do you add to a conversation? Be completely honest about your impact on others and their impact on you.

When your soul speaks, people around you get happier, more alive, and more energized. When your ego has the upper hand, the world around you diminishes its magnetic attraction and loses its glow. In my case, I had to admit that there was a tone of self-righteousness to many of my interactions with others that turned people off.

# Challenge What You Know

Curiosity opens up a new world of unexpected opportunities and wonder. It makes the impossible possible and conjures up what you imagine. With your rational mind, you keep magic at bay and what's more, you disconnect from your source, your heart, and your soul.

Kids live in a state of constant wonder. They approach their surroundings with a high level of curiosity and a minimum amount of knowledge. They don't expect things to happen a certain way, and they have no opinions or judgments. When they are really little, they don't even know that the fascinating object moving right in front of their eyes is their own hand.

When my youngest daughter was four or five, she loved to watch the movie *The NeverEnding Story*. One scene in particular kept her on the edge of her seat. In it, the protagonist, Atreyu, has to pass between two giant statues. He knows that he has to pass quickly or he'll die. My daughter watched this movie day after day and every time it came to this specific part, she would get scared and often she'd ask me, "Do you think he'll make it this time?" She had no experience of the movie being static. For her, it was a new adventure every time she watched.

Can you recall yourself being this unconditioned, experiencing life as a wonderful and mysterious adventure? Can you feel the thrill you got when doing something for the first time, not knowing how it would affect you; the excitement of learning to ride a bike or your first day at school?

I was at the beach the other day and saw a boy and a girl playing in the water, splashing around, digging their feet into the sand, and cheering with joy every time the water caught them. When their parents gathered them to leave, the little boy ran back to the shore and waved "Bye, bye, beach, bye, bye!"

Instances such as these allow you to get glimpses into your soul and help you remember yourself for who you really are.

Knowledge limits your outlook on life. It forces you to think in small and defined terms; it fosters expectations. You assume to feel a certain way when you wake up in the morning—and most likely that's what you'll get. You anticipate a line at the post office when dropping off a letter and, voilà, there it is. Over time, your expectations turn into habits and start to shape your reality and your perception of the world around you. You believe them to be the truth.

Every once in a while, however, the pattern is disrupted. All of a sudden, things turn out in surprisingly new ways and for a short moment, the veil of your day-to-day routine is lifted. Maybe you overslept and your whole morning unfolds completely different from other days. Or, maybe a volcano erupts and the trip you had been looking forward to for weeks is unexpectedly cancelled.

While these are all outside influences, there is yet another way of disrupting your expectations, and it's through awareness. If you look into your life and realize that most of your activities run on autopilot, you can consciously challenge your assumptions and create new and astonishing results.

## ACTION STEP

**Be aware of your expectations.** To change what you are expecting, you first need to be aware of your habits. Take a look around in your life and realize how your assumptions have secretly turned into ironclad facts.

**Challenge your expectations.** With more awareness, come new choices. Once you notice your expectations, challenge them. What if things can be different? Maybe you don't have to wake up in a grumpy mood every morning. Or, maybe there isn't a long line at the post office.

**Create more inspiring experiences.** Once you realize how much power you have in shaping your life by not knowing how it is going to unfold, you can consciously create outcomes that are more exciting. By not expecting disappointment, you are able to create fulfillment. By not expecting failure, you can create success.

When I lived in New York, women often told me that it was hard to find a good man in New York. The same happened when I lived in Los Angeles. According to general belief, it was impossible to find a good man in Los Angeles. I started to wonder whether good men were to be found anywhere.

Imagine being single in New York. It seems a bit silly, but let's pretend for a minute that it is impossible to find a good man, one that has all the attributes you are looking for in a city of eight million people. Do you realize how draining and demoralizing this belief is and how you are setting yourself up for a long and frustrating search?

Imagine again being single in New York. This time, you wake up every morning with the conviction that you can find your soulmate that same day; that he is out there somewhere, getting ready to go to work, buying a coffee, or hailing a cab.

Do you see the difference? By changing what's possible, you can create a more inspiring outcome.

# Relax & Let Go

*We cannot see our reflection in running water.*
*It is only in still water that we can see.*

— Taoist Proverb

One of the most important steps on your journey of self-discovery is to stop doing and to start being.

Remember the last time you were sick? Lying in bed without the strength to do anything? Your body ached, your head hurt, and even thinking was too much effort, let alone reading or watching a movie. You felt as if you'd never have the strength to get up again or perform a simple task.

Most likely, that's you at this point. Your whole system is on overload, your head is full of concepts and made-up dreams, your body hurts from the pressures of everyday life, your heart is numb, and you haven't listened to the voice of your soul in a long time. The last thing you need is to add more to your plate.

You are exhausted, and while your gut is telling you to relax and let go, your head is screaming to read more books, attend more lectures, set better goals, and figure out your future. It is telling you that kicking back is for losers and that following your gut has never worked out in the past. It's urging you that opportunities are waiting and that they might be lost if you don't grab them now.

What you are really listening to is the voice of fear; the fear of not working hard enough, of not being good enough, and of missing out on something. It is loud and it's convincing.

What you need at this point is the courage to ignore that voice in your head; be bold enough to do nothing and to wait for your natural desires to kick in. Just as when you were sick, after days and days of doing nothing, your spirit returned and you felt the urge to get up, watch a movie, or pick up a book.

The same will happen when you wake up to your sense of self. You come alive and a spark of desire is ignited.

For now, take the time to relax and to let go, do nothing for a while until your natural appetite to explore life starts to kick in. And just as feeling inspired seemed impossible when you were sick, seeing your sense of purpose at this point might appear as an unreachable goal.

If you were to explore right now what it is you want to do, not much good would come of it. It would be solely based on your exhaustion of a life lived under pressure.

Here and now, your job is to relax and let go. If a real desire stirs, follow it. If you feel like going to the movies, go to the movies. Even, or especially, if it's only 11 am. If you feel like lying down and sleeping, do that. Turn your life upside down and simply follow your aliveness. If you are tired, take a break; if you feel anxious, simply realize the feeling and do nothing about it. If you feel restless, go walk on the beach or in a park; if you feel sad, cry; and if you get angry, clean your house. Follow your own impulses, the ones leading you to more ease and well-being.

Many years ago, I had just started my business and was working hard to get it off the ground, I found myself at a dead end. I had discovered what I loved doing and the money was not following. As a matter of fact, the harder I tried, the more it went away. I had lost my job, I was broke, and I had two kids to feed. I told myself that losing my job was probably a blessing, as now I could dedicate myself to my passion 100 percent. I was making countless cold calls every day to little or no avail and was growing more desperate.

What was the missing ingredient? One day I just gave up trying and began doing nothing. Or better, I only did what I really wanted to do. My logic was this: "If I didn't get any results working hard all day, why not at least have a good time failing?"

What followed was astonishing. First, I slept; I slept a lot. As long as I was tired, I would not get up. I was determined to only do what was effortless. If getting up was hard, I wasn't getting up. Next, I watched movies. I really got into it. While other people went to work, I was watching the movies I had wanted to see for years. After that, I spent a lot of time in coffeehouses, enjoying myself and watching people.

I followed the flow and did what I wanted, but it wasn't easy. It was scary and it felt wrong. There was this constant voice in my head saying, "wrong, wrong, wrong! That's not how it works." And then there was this other part of me that I hadn't known before, and it wouldn't give in and was determined to live life differently.

After a few days, or maybe weeks, several things happened. I realized that the world was not caving in on me and I relaxed. It was an amazing experience. All the fear went away, the fear of not having control, the fear of being controlled, the fear of failing, of not failing, of having money, of not having money, and all of a sudden, it seemed that the whole world was available for me to play in.

I got curious. How did I want to live my life? What did I really want to do and how? I knew I loved working with people, but did I really want to make countless cold calls every day? Did I want to push hard and build a big business, or was it something more simple and gentle?

At that point, everything was possible. I did not know it at the time, but during those days, I learned to trust myself. I found my own timing, my rhythm, and started to follow the flow. I became the conductor of my own music. In the beginning, it felt uncomfortable letting go of old habits and beliefs, but over time, it became easier.

I realized which activities gave me energy and which ones didn't. Perception and awareness helped me to follow my heart rather than my head. I started making sound decisions, the ones that really worked for me. Life became effortless and light. Instead of making 100 calls to get two appointments, I made 20 calls and got 10. Money started to come in with more ease than ever before. I surrendered to my life and found my bliss.

I want you to do the same. Listen to life, tune into the universe, contemplate, surrender, and let it be. Get a sense of the tiny piece you are in the big scope of things and how your life wants to magically flow and fall into place. Stop pushing and start receiving. When you do get rushed, be aware of it and let it go; take a big breath and get back to your rhythm.

Do this and you just might discover that being your true self is effortless.

# Let It Happen—
# The Magic of Synchronicity

At this point of your journey, things will start to fall into place. Maybe you notice that some areas of your life flow with more ease than others. Some activities make you tense and others make you happy. Some people add energy to your life while others take away from it. Some thoughts light you up and some make you sad. You are observing the way you interact with the world. By putting your happiness first, you avoid instances that make you stressed.

With practice, two things are bound to happen. Your timing increases, things happen at the right place at the right time, and you experience more ease, even serendipity, and less pain. What does that mean? By following your inspiration, you start to attract different opportunities into your life.

Call it the Law of Attraction if you want, but it's really the laws of physics. Whatever you put out into the world is what's going to come back to you. If you add ease to your life, your life will get easier. If you do what makes you happy, you attract happiness. If you are angry, you attract people and situations that are irritating.

Ease comes from finding and following your own rhythm. When you relax into a flow that soothes and supports your timing, you start to create magic. This magic creates attraction. You'll be in tune with yourself.

The main characteristics of this state are a freedom of worry and effortlessness. Parking opens up right in front of you, the barista at your coffee shop doesn't charge you for your latte that morning, and you reach the client you have been trying to get in touch with all week. You are happy, you are relaxed, and life is the way it is supposed to be.

You can measure this by the number of serendipitous or synchronistic events that happen to you on any given day. The more you are following your life's path, the more things fall into place.

One of my clients made the decision to paint, something she had wanted to do for years. She told me that once she had made up her mind, art just showed up everywhere. She found a discarded, but well maintained, easel next to the dumpster when taking out the trash; the colors she wanted to buy at the art store were on sale; and one of her best friends called her to invite her to an art retreat that weekend. "It was weird," she told me, "almost as if the universe had been waiting for me to finally take action."

## ACTION STEP

Record the instances in your life that happen with complete ease. For example, traffic opens up when you are late for an appointment, your to-do list magically takes care of itself, a client calls to reschedule when you really need a break, etc. Make it a habit to write these events down every day. You will be surprised how often your life simply wants to work out.

You can also record hiccups and roadblocks. These are often hints to let you know that it's time to take a break or to slow down your pace. If these instances happen regularly, you might consider changing direction.

As I am writing this, a lady walks into the coffee shop where I am working on my laptop and sits down next to me. She pulls away the stool I have been using for my stuff and rests her feet on it. I was about to say, "Excuse me, lady, this is my chair," when I notice that I am hungry and it is time to leave. Just another subtle way of life telling me to take a break.

# Explore

After letting go, relaxing, and following your own rhythm, it's now time to start exploring. Remember our analogy of being sick? This is the phase when after days of resting, watching lots of movies, and indulging in doing nothing, you start to get an appetite for venturing out a little. You are not well enough to get back into the swing of things, but there is a sense of anticipation and curiosity; how has life changed while you were sick, what is everyone doing, did you miss anything?

With a fresh perspective, it's time to shake things up a little. So much in life is repetitive. We drive the same route to work, we get up at 7 a.m. sharp every morning, we buy what we know at the grocery store, and we order the same meal at our favorite restaurant.

While routines add stability to life, they also make it bland. We don't notice what's happening around us most of the time, we barrel down the highway without realizing how nature is changing, and often we take for granted that which is special and remarkable.

Curiosity can help you to stay alert and maintain a sense of wonder; looking for the deeper meaning in things and not taking life for granted is another way of keeping a fresh perspective. The other day I went to the doctor and got a prescription for an eye infection. I was supposed to pick it up at my local pharmacy, yet when I got there, they were out of the medication and couldn't get it before the next business day, which was a Monday. Three days to wait for my cream? I needed it now. I inquired if there was another pharmacy that carried it and was sent across town.

It was evening, the commute was a hassle, and it would have been easy to get frustrated and down on my luck. I decided, however, to make this trip fun. If life was orchestrated by a higher source, was there a purpose in this? Was I supposed to drive to the other end of town? The minute I asked myself that, I got intrigued. I took in every detail on my way to the pharmacy. I drove not the most convenient route but the one I liked best. I studied my environment and was totally engaged. By the time I had run my errand, I was happy and energized. The trip had given me time to take a break from the routine and the excuse to explore the world around me.

Are you ready to break up your routine and begin to envision your future? Use the following exercises to ignite your inspiration and creativity.

## ACTION STEP

1. **Make a Collage.** A great way to activate your imagination and explore your hidden desires is by making collages. This can be a single collage, for example, My Dream Life, or several different ones,

such as My Perfect Job, My Soulmate, or My Ideal Lifestyle. Make the collages as big or as small as you like. I use a big sketchpad that I fill with page after page of colorful pictures of how I envision my future. You can also use single sheets of paper that you frame and put up on your wall. Or, you can take a picture of your collage and put it on your computer desktop.

2. **Keep a Vision Journal.** Keeping a vision journal is an effective way to stimulate your imagination. You can carry it with you at all times and use it to write, paste, draw, and list everything that encompasses your aspirations and inspires your vision; the ideas that pop up in your head while you are stuck in traffic, the travel destinations that you have been thinking about for years, your wish to take an art class that you have been postponing for a long time; whatever ideas, images, desires, and thoughts intrigue and captivate you, they'll be captured in your vision journal.

3. **Brain Dump.** Take a notebook and pick a place where you will be undisturbed. Get comfortable, relax, and let your thoughts wander. When did you have the most fun in your life? What were you doing? Where did you live? Who were you with? Write this down. How about your current life? What are the things you enjoy most? What would you like

to do all the time, if you could? Do you like where you live? If not, what would be nicer? What lifestyle do you love? Who are the people you like spending time with? Again, write this down. Let your imagination run free. If you had a blank canvas and lots of colors, how would you draw your life?

4. **Change Your Look & Style.** I was 33 when I started to look for my true identity and began by changing my outer image. Up until then I had dressed in comfortable and self-knitted garb. All of a sudden, I became interested in mixing it up and sporting a more glamorous look. And because I do things all the way, I signed up for image-consulting training. In four weeks, I learned what colors looked best on me; what makeup to use and how to apply it; what shapes, forms, and styles brought out my body type, etc. I came home a changed person and started a fashion consulting business, showing other men and women how to dress and have fun with their clothes and bodies. Looking back, this was the beginning of my self-discovery and changed my life in more ways than I could know at the time.

Doing the various exercises and applying the transformation tools we explored, you should have glimpses of your true passions in life. In the next chapter,

"Design the Dream," we will take the process a step further and start designing your future life.

*Mantra*—On this part of your journey, your mantra is: "I don't know." Whenever your mind wants to limit your imagination, ask yourself "Why not?" Then, breathe, relax, and let go.

# CHAPTER 7
# Design the Dream

*There is no reason not to follow your heart.*

—**Steve Jobs,** *Stanford commencement address*

As you have seen, finding your true calling isn't that hard. As a matter of fact, the blueprint of who you are is already fully developed five months before you are born and is imprinted in your fingertips.

Once you know your personal gifts, a more complex question arises: *How do you translate your unique abilities and talents into your life and work?*

Let's say you discovered that you are a passionate communicator who loves adventures. There are many different ways to actualize these gifts: you could be a public speaker, a salesperson, a writer who travels the world, a politician, even a singer . . . all different ways to express your talent of persuasive communication.

Or, if you are a life coach, like me, you can use your skills to communicate passionately with your clients, persuade them to live happier lives while satisfying your hunger for adventure by traveling the globe teaching life-changing seminars.

Once you know your life purpose, there are a number of ways to express it. This is where the ability to be sensitive to your needs and to find out what lights you up comes in as a crucial measurement tool. Your sensory awareness will tell you whether you want to use your skills to talk to big crowds, write novels, sing, paint, or express yourself in other ways.

Getting the details right is crucial not only in pursing your passion but also in designing your ideal lifestyle. In the following sections I show you how to take the discoveries you made so far and turn them into a life map and ultimately into a plan for action. Only when you actively apply your unique talents will your entire life move in the direction you desire.

## Assemble the Pieces

Let's design your dream by taking the pieces of your puzzle, the parts of what you love doing and assembling them into your ideal lifestyle, a possible business project, and your future vision.

If you haven't yet done the puzzle exercise from Chapter 5, "What Lights You Up?" I recommend you do it now before you venture on.

In the following section, I will show you two examples of using your puzzle to start outlining your dream. I will demonstrate step by step how to take the different pieces and organize them into three life sections: your expression (vocation), your nature (essence), and your lifestyle (community, health, and recreation).

## Example One: Sarah's Puzzle

When Sarah started working with me, she had a fulltime job as a marketing director for a software company. She liked her job because it provided her with a good income and it was a career opportunity. She knew, however, that working 9–5 wasn't her long-term goal and that marketing wasn't her real passion. It was simply something she was good at. What she really wanted was to start her own business.

After working with Sarah for a few weeks, it became clear that she had a special gift of expressing herself through words and that she was highly creative. Her gentle and unpretentious way drew people in and her enjoyment of playing with fabric, colors, and texture translated into beautiful pieces of art.

While she loved traveling and interacting with people, she knew that solitude and having a sanctuary was essential to her well-being.

Below you see Sarah's puzzle. It reflects her love for expressing herself through art and a desire for a mindful and simple lifestyle that allows lots of room for creation.

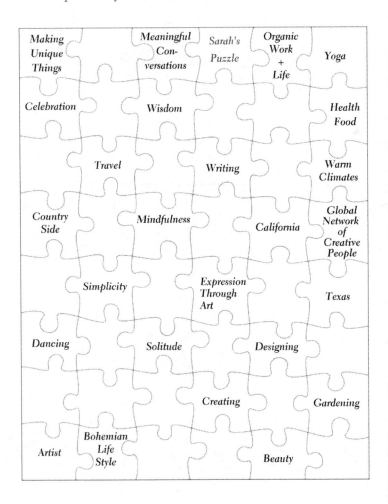

To organize the pieces, let's divide them into three categories:

1. **Sarah's Expression**
   Simplicity
   Beauty
   Mindfulness
   Making unique things
   Expression through art
   Travel
   Creating
   Writing
   Dancing
   Designing
   Gardening
   Celebration
   Meaningful conversations

2. **Sarah's Nature**
   Simplicity
   Beauty
   Mindfulness
   Creating
   Expression through art
   Bohemian lifestyle
   Wisdom
   Artist
   Solitude

3.  **Sarah's Lifestyle**
    Simplicity
    Beauty
    Mindfulness
    Bohemian lifestyle
    Making unique things
    Travel
    Global network of creative people
    Countryside
    Gardening
    Health food
    Organic work + life
    California
    Texas
    Yoga

To make working with the various pieces easier, we place them in three circles, one for each category.

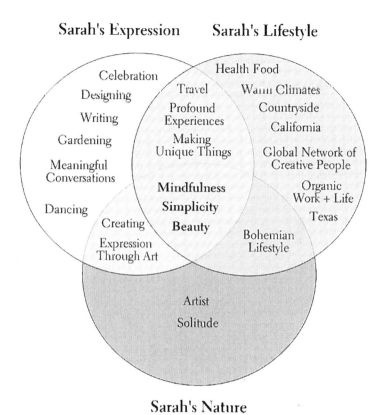

**Sarah's Expression**  **Sarah's Lifestyle**

Celebration

Designing

Writing

Gardening

Meaningful
Conversations

Dancing

Creating

Expression
Through Art

Travel

Profound
Experiences

Making
Unique Things

**Mindfulness**

**Simplicity**

**Beauty**

Health Food

Warm Climates

Countryside

California

Global Network of
Creative People

Organic
Work + Life

Texas

Bohemian
Lifestyle

Artist

Solitude

**Sarah's Nature**

You might have noticed that some of the puzzle pieces show up in more than one category. Simplicity, mindfulness, and beauty, for example, are present in each one. This tells us that simplicity, mindfulness, and beauty are an essential part of Sarah's life. In order to keep a healthy balance, she has to make sure those ingredients are present in her daily life.

Sarah had a good idea about her ideal lifestyle. She wanted to live in the countryside, be part of a global network of creative people, and create an organic work-life balance. She was effervescing with ideas and we got right to work.

Maybe you are not there yet—and that is absolutely fine. In the second example you will see that even without having the slightest idea about your life purpose, you can use the puzzle exercise to make important distinctions and get started in the right direction.

REMINDER

Finding out why you are here isn't hard. You can use the steps outlined in this book or hire a good coach to help you—but NOTHING will change until you apply what you've discovered and translate it to action steps.

I really want you to get this, because it's where the road divides—into the people who take life and turn it into an exciting adventure and those who don't.

Do you know that most people who discover their true nature do nothing about it? It's one thing to take a job at Starbucks, something you don't really care about, and a completely different matter to work at something that's close to your heart. For some strange reason, the things you really want to do, the ones directly connected to your soul, are the ones you are most afraid of.

Imagine being told that you are not a good barista. You probably just shrug your shoulders and think, who cares? But if people tell you that your writing lacks finesse or that your art isn't touching them, you are crushed. By pursuing your dream, you put everything on the line—or at least that's how it feels—which is the reason most people avoid the experience at all cost. They'd rather die with the music still in them, than apply themselves to something that deeply touches their soul.

Here is the paradox: whatever you love doing, you will be excellent at it. But, you can't be certain until you try.

I recommend you take baby steps to get there. Your first public speech might not be flawless, but with a little practice and effort, you will become better. Michael Jackson, for example, was a natural born dancer; it was his relentless practice, however, that turned him into an awe-inspiring performer.

In Sarah's case, she started to create and sell her art. She designed an online shopping portal, met with local boutique owners, who commissioned her work, and displayed her art at a weekly outdoor market where she met many new customers.

All it required was taking a few simple steps.

## Example Two: Karin's Puzzle
Let's use another example. This time I work with my own puzzle, the one I created when I first started on my journey of self-discovery.

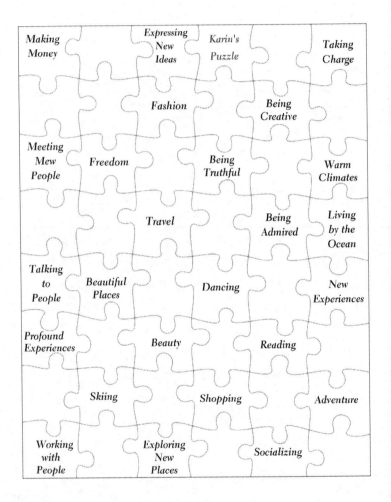

Contrary to Sarah, who had already created a lifestyle that combined a lot of the elements that made her happy, I was completely in the dark about my true desires and personal strengths.

Dividing the pieces into three categories, we come up with the following design:

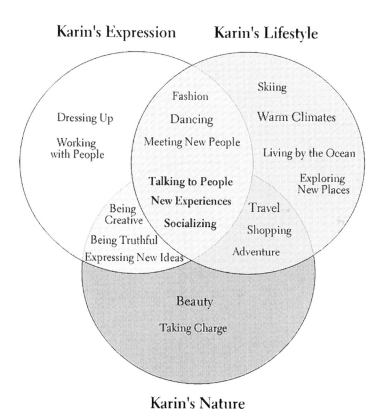

**Karin's Expression**     **Karin's Lifestyle**

Fashion

Skiing

Dressing Up     Dancing     Warm Climates

Working with People     Meeting New People

Living by the Ocean

Talking to People     Exploring New Places

New Experiences

Being Creative     Socializing     Travel

Being Truthful     Shopping

Expressing New Ideas     Adventure

Beauty

Taking Charge

**Karin's Nature**

When I first did this exercise, I was a homemaker and I had just started a small business as a fashion consultant on the side. While I did not know my unique talents, I realized that I liked working with people, that I had a passion for travel, and that making money was fun. I had an eye for beauty, an interest in new experiences, and a thirst for adventure.

Finding the pieces of my puzzle gave me the courage to integrate more of the things I enjoyed into my life. I got over feeling shy in front of people and started to give presentations for my fashion-consulting business. I went out to socialize and to meet people. I embraced new opportunities, which helped my business to grow. In the process, I made more money and had more fun.

Eventually all the pieces of my puzzle started to fall into place. I met my mentor, who helped me to develop my talent of reading people; I embraced opportunities to travel and I had a blast meeting new clients all over the world. In time, I moved to the United States, a dream I had harbored since I was a young girl, and grew my business on a global level.

*What if you don't want to start a business or change your life?* What if you don't want to leave a stable job or move to an exotic new country?

Here is the good news: you don't have to. After finding your talents, you can simply integrate them into your life without disrupting the flow at all.

Remember Ben from Chapter 1, who at 15 found out that he had a passion for music, something he had missed out on his whole life? He did not start a career as a rock star or leave his job. He pursued his love for music in simpler and more inclusive ways. He bought a guitar and took lessons, he started to take an active part in his local church choir, and once he knew how to play, he and his son, who it turned out also loved to play the guitar, started to jam together. In the process, Ben became happier and more fulfilled than he had ever been. He had found what he was missing.

## Your Dream in Action

If you did the puzzle exercise and assembled your pieces, you should now have a lot of material with which you can work.

Look at all the different pieces and ask yourself, What is it that wants to emerge? What patterns do I see? How do the different pieces fit together? What step or steps can I take today that will get me closer to where I want to be?

While doing this exercise, one of my clients realized that what she wanted most was to find a husband and to start a jewelry business. At the time, she was working as a sales rep for an insurance company, a job she hated. She decided it was time to take action and go for her dream. She started a project to find a husband. She really went for it and searched for a man online and off. Eventually, she found a wonderful partner and together they moved to a place that was her perfect environment. She also left her job and started a jewelry business which grew quickly using her sales and marketing skills to promote it.

To get going on your own dream, select a few pieces from your puzzle for a simple project. This can be anything from throwing a dinner party to starting a blog, finding a husband, writing a book, learning how to make cupcakes, or anything else that inspires you. It does not matter how crazy your idea is, as long as you are excited about it.

The important part about this stage is to *take immediate action*. Have you ever noticed how easy it is to get distracted from something you feel really inspired about? If you don't take action right away, your idea fades into the background until you forget about it all together.

Another crucial point is to *take simple, easy steps*. Time and again, I have seen people get so overwhelmed with launching a project that they never start. Next, be aware of the voices in your head telling you things such as, "Oh, this will probably never work." or "There are already so many people out there doing this." or "I am not good at this." or "I need to get a degree, certification, or credit before I can start," etc. It's your fear talking and you'll do best not to listen to it and just keep going.

Every good project has a beginning, a middle, and an end—in addition to a timeline. Let's imagine for the purpose of this book that eating healthy is a passion of yours. You have taken many classes and attended nutrition seminars and have read numerous books on the topic. While doing your puzzle exercise, you realized that you'd love to turn your passion for food into a more active part of your life.

Here are the three steps you can take immediately to turn your passion into a project and eventually into a business.

Please note that this is a simplified outline. It would go beyond the purpose of this book to teach you business skills in depth. There are many excellent books on how to build a small business, a few of which I have added to the reading list in the Appendix at the end of this book.

## ACTION STEPS

**Part One:** Find out as much as you can about the health-food business. Search the Internet, read blogs, talk to other food aficionados, etc. Is there a demand for this type of service? How could you set up a project or business in this field? What available options are there?

What would be fun and enjoyable for you? For example, do you see yourself organizing cooking classes, do you want to work with people's health on a personal level, do you want to become a nutritional consultant, or even a chef? As a rule of thumb, give yourself three or four weeks for this stage.

**Part Two:** If you are certain that this is what you want to pursue, start learning your craft. Attend classes or seminars, connect with other like-minded people, or put together classes for a nutritional consultant. You can also create a website or start your own blog about the subject. Depending on the learning curve, part two might take several weeks, months, or even years. In my experience, you never feel quite ready to move on, so don't spend too much time perfecting your craft. You always keep learning.

**Part Three:** Put what you learned into action. For example, put together your own small cooking class or nutritional seminar. This can be as simple as asking a friend to organize a cooking event at her house, offering a nutrition class at a community center, or showing people one-on-one how to develop healthier eating habits. At this point, start charging a small fee for your service.

This is a simple example of how to start a passion project. You can do this while having a job, working regular hours, or taking care of your family.

## Stay on Course

Life is determined to pull you off track at all times, especially if you set out to do something extraordinary. Your mom will try to talk you out of it, your friends will get jealous, and your kids will think you are crazy—so look out for those subtle, or not-so-subtle, distractions and find ways to keep your vision alive.

**Focus your attention.** Whatever you focus on expands. How you use your attention will make the difference between loving your project or worrying about every little detail of it. If you consistently think about everything that can go wrong and whether things will work out or not, you won't enjoy the project nearly as much, plus it will go slower.

If you use your attention wisely, you can navigate through life with pleasure and ease, choosing experiences that you enjoy. If you focus on ease, that's what you get. It will expand your perceptions and make your experiences magical. If you focus on problems, they too will invade your life.

**Form a support team.** Do you know others who are working on a business or project? I recommend forming a mastermind group and setting up weekly meetings to check in, set goals, report on your progress, and cheer one another on. This is invaluable in keeping your project alive and staying focused. *It will give you a sounding board to try out ideas, get feedback, and find the support you need to succeed.*

**To-do lists.** Knowing what you are doing each day will help you to stay focused. Personally, I love writing my to-do list every night. Checking things off the next day increases my drive and gives me energy. Beware of being too hard on yourself. Your list is a guideline; your project is a game. Have fun with it.

**Set weekly and daily goals.** Goals give your project direction and purpose. They'll tell you where you are going. It's crucial that goals inspire you without being overwhelming. Goals can be the juice that keeps your project together and helps you to stay focused and monitor your progress.

Last, but not least, remember to enjoy what you are doing and to be proud of your achievements.

# Be Bold

It takes courage to leave the beaten path and to follow your own truth. It means to step into unknown and uncharted territory. In most cases, it means change.

Change creates anxiety, and anxiety creates the urge for control. And yet, at this point, the only way forward is to embrace the changes and to relax into uncertainty. You have to let go of control and knowing; otherwise you keep recreating your old life all over again.

You are starting to see who you truly are, what you want and how magical your life can be. Hold on to this vision, as it will help you to take bold leaps. Knowing your path generates a sense of deep self-trust; it gives you the courage to relax into this new world of paradox and complexity. If you can embrace the fact that you don't have (nor need) all the answers and that most of your fears are not based in reality, you can find a way to a better life.

Forget about doing the right thing; don't worry about what others think. Be creative, think big, and do what makes you happy. There is not one way, one answer, or one road to take. You can create anything you want any way you want to. The only requirement is that it inspires you. If it moves you, it will move others too. *Charting your own path makes you magnetic.*

# Develop New Habits

It is important to realize that while you are building your new life, your old one will try to keep you in a tight grip. This might show up in the form of self-sabotage or a stubborn refusal to change unproductive habits. While these are common growing pains, it is something to be acutely aware of. On the brink of success, I have seen people get scared, make bad decisions, or quit.

To avoid this, become aware of any unproductive habits and replace them with ones that are more effective. For example, learn to acknowledge your achievements instead of complaining to your friends about your failures; replace the habit of doubting yourself with the ability of setting and meeting exciting goals; learn to think positive instead of always expecting the worst in life; and, replace your pesky habit of shutting down anything fun with the bold ability of expecting and attracting only the best.

If not replaced, your old routines will make it impossible for you to change your ways—and your outcome in life.

How do you change a habit?

ACTION STEP

Distinguish a habit your want to change; your need to complain, for example, or your habit of gossiping, criticizing, blaming, etc. Next, pick a habit or trait you would like to have instead, a positive attitude, for example, the ability to acknowledge others, of being more generous, etc.

Now, ask yourself if there is anybody who embodies the trait you want to adopt. This can be a friend, a mentor, a movie star, or any other person you know. How do they display the habit you want to adopt? How do they keep a positive attitude? How do they express their appreciation and love for life?

Your next step consists of embracing this new way of approaching life and to model after the person you chose as your role model. You might feel awkward and clumsy at first, almost as if you are faking it (which you are), but over time you will let go of your old habit and begin to incorporate the new one. Don't think it's possible? Read on to find out how I changed from a serious know-it-all to a cheerful dancing queen.

Growing up, I had developed a habit of being overly serious that as an adult pervaded my whole being. This didn't really bother me until I moved to Austin, Texas. Boy, were things different there. People were smiling all day long in a BIG way and my serious mood was most unusual. It was especially noticeable every time I went out to dance and have a good time. While other women were asked on the dance floor all night long, few men approached me and if they did, it was only once.

I was clueless to why this happened and convinced myself that men did not like me very much. I talked to one of my girlfriends about it and she simply told me to lighten up and to be a bit more cheerful. "Well," I replied, "that's just not who I am." Her response was, "Oh, just fake it then."

I was confused. What in the world was she thinking? How could I fake something so foreign to my true nature? Surely, nobody would buy my act. Nevertheless, the next time out on the town, I tried it. Equipped with a strawberry Margarita, I put a big (fake) smile on my face. Sure enough, a handsome Texan fellow asked me to dance. I kept smiling—and dancing—all night long.

I was shocked. Men even told me that I was a lot of fun. "What? They bought it?" I couldn't believe it. Yet, encouraged through the feedback, I kept up my act until it became second nature. I learned to genuinely enjoy myself and realized that being playful was closer to who I was than my old serious self.

I put together a list of habits that I adopted and that have proven to be crucial in keeping my vision strong and my dream inspired. Try them out and see if they work for you. If they do, keep them; if they don't, discard them. In addition, make your own list of positive habits and start to integrate them, one by one, into your life.

This is an exciting part of your journey. By actively adding new elements, you can alter the way you live your life and experience the world around you.

**Keep a Positive Attitude.** Staying positive is one of the most important habits you can develop, if not *the* most important one. We are surrounded by negativity all day long—just turn on the news or open a newspaper and you'll understand what I mean. It takes awareness and discipline to stay positive and to follow through on your choices.

The best way to do this is by focusing on your vision and by stepping into action to realize your dream. Actively doing what you love is one of the best ways to stay clear of worries, negative thoughts, and stressful emotions. Positive action keeps you healthy, productive, and out of your head. This requires being attentive to your environment to avoid getting pulled into negative thoughts or emotions.

One of my clients realized that more than anything she loved planning and preparing exquisite meals. She also took a lot of joy in setting tables and creating magical environments for others, so she decided to start a supper club. The days leading up to her first event were excruciating. She kept revising her plan and going through her to-do lists. She called me almost every day to tell me that she didn't think the event was a good idea, that it probably would not turn out well, and that she thought it would be best to cancel it and forget about the whole idea.

Good thing she had a coach.

A few days before her supper party, she moved into high gear. She started to shop, prepare and cook first dishes, assemble decorations, write place cards, arrange flowers, and pick her dinner music. She was ecstatic and all her fears and worries had disappeared.

Her event was a smashing success. Yes, she forgot to play the music the night of the party and one of her dishes didn't turn out as she wished, but she was the only one to notice, while everyone else had a wonderful time.

The same is true for *your* gifts and passions. They come to life when you apply them. They enchant you in action. As a matter of fact, they are your ticket to staying on the positive path. So, instead of worrying about how to best use your greatness, be bold and step right into it. Once you do, your fears will dissipate.

**Surround yourself with positive people.** Do you know how to reenergize a magnet that has lost its power? You connect it to another, stronger magnet. The same is true for your own power. To stay inspired and positive, surround yourself with inspiring and positive people.

**Read inspiring books and articles.** Whenever I lose my focus or start on a downward spiral, I pick up a book or read an article that reenergizes me and shifts my attention. I listen to books while I am driving, exercising, or walking on the beach. It keeps my focus clear and my spirits high. I recommend you start a library and playlist of your favorite authors and bloggers that you can tap into any time you need inspiration.

**Keep a spiritual practice.** Keeping a spiritual practice helps you to stay grounded and connected to the higher purpose of your existence. Maybe you like to meditate, belong to a church, or practice yoga. No matter what your practice, taking time out for yourself will help you to tap into the universal love surrounding you and give you the courage to keep forging your path.

**Exercising** and **eating healthy** are two more habits that have a positive impact on how you feel and how you experience the world. Nothing will change your mood faster than a walk on the beach or a bike ride in nature. At least in my book it does. If you haven't exercised in a while, I recommend you join a group or hire a personal trainer.

Carlos hadn't exercised in several years and the loss of strength started to have a real impact on his life. He noticed that he was in a low mood more often than he cared for and that the slightest physical effort exhausted him. He also told me that he and his wife used to dance the night away and that he just couldn't do it anymore.

We looked at options for him to get back into shape and he committed to hire a personal trainer for a month. It changed his whole life. Not only did his mood improve, his body changed and he had more strength do all the things he had been missing out on. Hiking and biking on the weekends, playing soccer with his kids, and most of all, taking his wife dancing again.

These are just a few of the habits that have helped me in creating a happier and more fulfilling lifestyle. Keep experimenting with the ones that work for you and remember that it takes patience and practice to stay on the positive path.

## Count Your Blessings

*Gratitude unlocks the fullness of life. It turns what we have into enough, and more. It turns denial into acceptance, chaos to order, confusions to clarity. It can turn a meal into a feast, a house into a home, a stranger into a friend. Gratitude makes sense of our past, brings peace for today, and creates a vision for tomorrow.*

—**Melody Beattie,** *The Language of Letting Go*

There is one more secret ingredient you need to continue on your path of happiness and to enjoy an enchanted life: *gratitude.*

Be grateful for what you have. Appreciate your friendships. Take time to cherish your accomplishments. Be grateful to be alive.

Gratitude is the number one ingredient that people attribute to their happiness and success. Hard work, discipline, consistency, and dedication are important factors in accomplishing anything. But gratitude, deep and profound appreciation for what you have and for who you are, is one of the secret ingredients to a fulfilled and happy life.

**Gratitude gives you power.** It makes you strong. It's the difference between being the victim of your circumstances and taking responsibility for your life. Feeling appreciation instead of blame, thankfulness instead of resentment. It's a choice we make every instance of our lives.

**Gratitude makes you healthy.** It opens your heart. It makes you happier and puts a spark into your eyes. Practicing grateful thinking reaps emotional, physical, and interpersonal benefits. People who regularly keep a gratitude journal report fewer illness symptoms, feel better about their lives as a whole, and are more optimistic about the future.

**Put gratitude first.** Find things to be grateful for now and don't wait for something amazing to happen in your life later. It's a shift of awareness, from outward to inward, from looking for fault in the world out there to finding the power of love inside you.

*Mantra*—Creating and putting together your dream life can be overwhelming. Your mantra at this point is to keep it simple. Take one step at a time. If you can't see the next part of your journey, don't worry. Each step will reveal itself at the right place and at the right time. Trust the journey. Your life is supposed to work out.

# FINAL THOUGHTS

Welcome to the end of the life as you know it—and welcome to the end of this book. If you have been hanging in, congratulations, you now have the steps and practical tools to find your true calling, understand what you are put on this Earth to do, and live your wildest dream!

In this book, you discovered that you were born a unique human being, equipped with a set of distinctive qualities and skills that only you possess. You learned the secrets that prevent you from understanding your own life purpose—and found ways to discover and tap into your personal talents. You were handed a set of transformational tools and you discovered that you have a clearly defined path, a purpose that is given to you at birth. You also looked at the obstacles that have the power to stop you from following your legend and ways to avoid them.

*Now it is time to put your discoveries into action and to create the life you are thrilled to live.*

Start with some simple exercises from this book. Make a collage, start a vision journal, or sign up for my blog to receive weekly inspirations that will keep you on track and help you chart your course.

If you keep up your practice of self-discovery, incorporate into your life the activities that bring you alive, develop new habits, and stay on the positive path, you will see the changes you desire.

You deserve to have everything you ever wanted. All you need is the courage to take the first step. The rest is going to be an exhilarating ride.

# APPENDIX

## Worksheet 1
## Open-Ended Questions

1. What do you want?

2. If you knew what you wanted, what would it be?

3. What makes you happy?

4. What did you do at a time in your life when you were really happy? Where did you live? Who were you with?

5. What is your heart's desire?

6. What brings you most joy?

7. What is fun for you?

8. What do you love doing?

9. How do you like to spend your time?

10. When are you most relaxed?

11. What activities make you forget time?

12. What are you doing in the moments when you forget time?

13. If you could do anything and you couldn't fail, what would it be?

14. What are the things you always wanted to do but haven't?

15. If you could design your life from scratch, what would it look like?

16. If you had only one more year to live, how would you spend it?

17. If you did not have to work, what would you do?

18. Where do you want to live?

19. What do you like about your current job?

20. In what business would you like to be involved in?

21. What activities interest you?

22. What relaxes you?

23. What do you add to the world?

24. What is special about you? How are you different?

25. What is missing from your life?

26. What are your talents?

27. What do you do when time does not matter?

28. What would you do if money didn't matter?

29. What do you like to do most?

30. If you were extremely rich, what work would you do?

31. If you were extremely rich, how would you spend your time?

32. What is your unique quality?

33. What are the things that people admire about you?

34. What comes natural to you?

35. What are you the Picasso of? What are you a master in?

36. What would make you want to play and be active all day?

37. What activities raise your vitality?

38. What makes you laugh?

39. What would be the most enjoyable way to make money?

40. When you have so much fun that you lose your mind, what are you doing?

41. What is your passion?

42. What are you passionate about?

43. What excites you?

44. How excited are you on a scale from 1 to 10? What would make it a 10?

45. When is your heart in ecstasy?

46. If you could be totally outrageous or wild, what would you do?

47. What would make you take the plunge?

48. What's your dream?

49. If your life was a dream, what would you do?

50. If you had financial freedom, what would you do?

51. When are you happiest?

# Worksheet 2
# Puzzle Exercise Template

# Worksheet 3
# Rate Your Level of Aliveness —
# Weekly Tracker

| Days | In the Morning | | In the Afternoon | | In the Evening | |
|---|---|---|---|---|---|---|
| | My Number (1 - 10) | My Sensation | My Number (1 - 10) | My Sensation | My Number (1 - 10) | My Sensation |
| Monday | | | | | | |
| Tuesday | | | | | | |
| Wednesday | | | | | | |
| Thursday | | | | | | |
| Friday | | | | | | |
| Saturday | | | | | | |
| Sunday | | | | | | |

# Reading List

Agassi, Andre. *Open: An Autobiography.* New York: AKA Publishing, 2009.

Beattie, Melody. *The Language of Letting Go: Hazelden Meditation Series.* Center City, Minnesota: Hazelden Publishing, 1998.

Beck, Martha. *Finding Your Own North Star: Claiming the Life You Were Meant to Live.* New York: Three Rivers Press, 2001.

Branson, Richard. *Losing My Virginity: How I've Survived, Had Fun, and Made a Fortune Doing Business My Way.* New York: Three Rivers Press, 1998.

Branson, Richard. *Screw It, Let's Do It: Lessons in Life.* London: Virgin Books, 2006.

Chopra, Deepak. *Reinventing the Body, Resurrecting the Soul: How to Create a New You.* New York: Harmony, 2009.

Chopra, Deepak. *The Spontaneous Fulfillment of Desire: Harnessing the Infinite Power of Coincidence.* New York: Harmony, 2003.

Chopra, Deepak. *The Ultimate Happiness Prescription: 7 Keys to Joy and Enlightenment.* New York: Harmony, 2009.

Coelho, Paolo. *The Alchemist.* New York: HarperCollins, 1993.

Coelho, Paolo. *Brida.* New York: HarperCollins, 2008.

Erickson, Gary. *Raising the Bar: Integrity and Passion in Life and Business: The Story of Cliff Bar Inc.* San Francisco: Jossey-Bass, 2004.

Ferrazzi, Keith and Tahl Raz. *Never Eat Alone, Expanded and Updated: And Other Secrets to Success, One Relationship at a Time.* New York: Crown Business, 2014.

Frankl, Viktor E. *Man's Search for Meaning.* New York: Pocket Books, 2000.

Gelb, Michael J. *How to Think Like Leonardo da Vinci: Seven Steps to Genius Every Day.* New York: Delacorte Press, 1998.

Godin, Seth. *Linchpin: Are You Indispensable?* New York: Portfolio, 2010.

Guillebeau, Chris. *The $100 Startup: Reinvent the Way You Make a Living, Do What You Love, and Create a New Future.* New York: Crown Business, 2012.

Hill, Napoleon. *Think and Grow Rich.* Radford, Virginia: Wilder Publications, 2007.

Huffington, Arianna. *Thrive: The Third Metric to Redefining Success and Creating a Life of Well-Being, Wisdom, and Wonder.* New York: Harmony, 2014.

Kashdan, Todd B. *Curious? Discover the Missing Ingredient to a Fulfilling Life.* New York: HarperCollins, 2009.

LaPorte, Danielle. *The Desire Map: A Guide to Creating Goals with Soul.* Boulder, Colorado: Sounds True, 2014.

Myss, Caroline. *Anatomy of the Spirit: The Seven Stages of Power and Healing.* New York: Harmony, 1996.

Myss, Caroline. *Sacred Contracts: Awakening Your Divine Potential.* New York: Harmony, 2002.

Roddick, Anita. *Body and Soul: Profits with Principles— The Amazing Success Story of Anita Roddick & The Body Shop.* New York: Crown, 1991.

Rodriguez, Robert. *Rebel Without a Crew: Or How a 23-Year-Old Filmmaker With $7,000 Became a Hollywood Player.* New York: Plume, 1996.

Ruiz, Don Miguel. *The Four Agreements: A Practical Guide to Personal Freedom.* San Rafael, California: Amber-Allen Publishing, 1997.

Ruiz, Don Miguel. *The Mastery of Love: A Practical Guide to the Art of Relationship.* San Rafael, California: Amber-Allen Publishing, 1999.

Seligman, Martin E. P. *Authentic Happiness: Using the New Positive Psychology to Realize Your Potential for Lasting Fulfillment.* New York: Free Press, 2002.

Slim, Pamela. *Body of Work: Finding the Thread, That Ties Your Story Together.* New York: Portfolio, 2013.

Tracy, Brian. *Flight Plan: The Real Secret of Success.* San Francisco: Berrett-Koehler, 2008.

White, Robert. *Living an Extraordinary Life—Unlocking Your Potential for Success, Joy and Fulfillment.* Extraordinary Resources (third edition), 2005.

# Photo Credits

*Picture 1*—"Amelia's Pretty Blue Eyes" by Donnie Ray Jones via Flickr under a Creative Commons License: https://www.flickr.com/photos/donnieray.

*Picture 2*—"Lola 2" by Anthony Kelly via Flickr under a Creative Commons License: https://www.flickr.com/photos/62337512@N00.

*Picture 3*—"Conrad black and white" by Anthony Kelly via Flickr under a Creative Commons License: https://www.flickr.com/photos/62337512@N00.

*Pictures 4 and 5*—From the author's collection.

# ABOUT THE AUTHOR

Karin is the founder and president of Karin Lehmann International, a company dedicated to assisting people in creating lives of electric abundance and happiness. Using the cellular transformation tools she teaches, Karin has changed her own life from living in a small village in Germany to being one of the top coaches for women.

Recognized as an expert in her field for her ability to laser in on a person's unique qualities, she has helped thousands of people in building their dream lives, finding their ideal partners, and creating lucrative businesses they love.

Today, after 20 years in the consulting and mentoring field, Karin enjoys conducting workshops, seminars, and personal consulting sessions in Europe and the United States, showing people how to use their brilliance to create passionate lifestyles, relationships, and careers.

Karin is a mother of three and lives in Ventura, California, with her husband and youngest daughter.

To find out more about Karin and to sign up for her weekly newsletter, please visit her website at http://karinlehmann.com.

51763288R00114

Made in the USA
Charleston, SC
03 February 2016